The RABBI & The NUNS

*The Inside Story of a Rabbi's Therapeutic Work
with the Sisters of St. Francis*

RABBI DR. ABRAHAM J. TWERSKI, M.D.

MEKOR PRESS

© 2013 by Mekor Press, a division of Menucha Publishers
Typeset and designed by Beena Sklare
All rights reserved

ISBN 978-1-61465-133-8

No part of this publication may be translated, reproduced, stored in a retrieval system, or transmitted in any form or by any means, electronic, mechanical, photocopying, recording, or otherwise, without prior permission in writing from both the copyright holder and the publisher.

Distributed by Menucha Publishers
250 44th Street
Brooklyn, NY 11232
Tel/Fax: 718-232-0856
www.mekorpress.com

Printed in Israel

CONTENTS

Introduction 7

1	Rabbi Becomes Physician.................................	9
2	Breaking the Chain..	15
3	The Lebanese Rescuer.......................................	17
4	Medical Internship..	20
5	A Humbling Experience...................................	26
6	My Mother's Contribution...............................	31
7	The Nucleus Within..	35
8	St. Francis General Hospital.............................	41
9	Meeting the Bishop...	47
10	The Cardinal's Aspirations................................	50
11	The Pope's Mitzvah...	52
12	Obedience...	54
13	My Relationship with the Sisters.....................	56
14	Variations in Psychotherapy.............................	59
15	Delusion and Reality	67
16	Good Habits...	71
17	Two Fascinating Cases	74
18	More Real than Reality.....................................	79
19	A Non-narcotic Painkiller	81
20	Mind-Body Relationship	83
21	Not Mentally Ill...	86
22	I'm Not Angry..	88
23	Know Your Skills	93
24	A Serious Regret..	95

25	The Fugitive	97
26	Guilt	100
27	Kleptomania	102
28	Obedience versus Control	104
29	Challenge of Faith I	107
30	Challenge of Faith II	110
31	Let Go and Let G-d	113
32	The Pain of Growth	116
33	Humility	119
34	Thank G-d I'm a Psychiatrist	123
35	Ignorance of Addiction	130
36	Misguided Kindness	133
37	Touchless Hugging	135
38	The Flying Nun	137
39	Medical Addiction: A Nun's Story	143
40	A Priest's Story	147
41	Wayward Priest	152
42	There Is No Immunity	154
43	A Committee Plan	157
44	The Self-Esteem Issue	159
45	Identity	163
46	Spirituality and Religion	165
47	The Birth of Gateway	171
48	A United Effort	174
49	What I Learned	176
50	The Rabbinic Influence	187
	About the Author	191

INTRODUCTION

IF THE TITLE OF THIS BOOK aroused your curiosity, that is what it was intended to do. A long-term relationship between an Orthodox rabbi and nuns is a bit unusual. When I walked down the street in the company of the sisters, many heads turned in disbelief.

This was a unique relationship that lasted for twenty years. I will try to depict the nature of that association and provide some autobiographical information that may explain how the connection came about and why it was so successful.

World history is replete with tragedies wrought by religious differences. I believe that attributing disagreements, wars, and the inability to coexist peacefully to religious differences is nothing but rationalization, an invoking of religion to explain away hostility and selfishness that stems from totally different sources. Religious differences serve as a convenient scapegoat, and one tries to justify one's aggression or violation of the rights of others by ascribing one's motivation to defense of one's religion.

The relationship of the church to Jews throughout history

was very thorny. I knew it, the bishop knew it, and the sisters knew it. However, we were working on being of service to humanity, and our feelings about the past were not going to deter us from our determination to work together. Thus, the unique experience of "the rabbi and the nuns" set an important example of what can be if you want it to be.

This was a very rewarding experience for all of us. Hopefully, the nuns benefited from our treatment. I know that we benefited immensely from the relationship.

1
RABBI BECOMES PHYSICIAN

You might wonder, How did this all come about? How did an Orthodox Chassidic rabbi become involved in treating nuns and priests?

Truth is stranger than fiction. It was a superb combination for over twenty years. One of its results was a major alcohol and drug treatment system that now ministers to eighteen hundred clients daily.

A bit of background information is necessary to make any sense of this book.

I was groomed to become a rabbi and succeed my father in the congregation he had established. I was ordained in 1951 and began serving as his assistant.

My father was an intuitive therapist, and his study was constantly buzzing until the wee hours of the morning with people seeking his counsel on a variety of problems. His Solomonic wisdom was sought by people from all walks of life, Jewish and non-Jewish. My father arbitrated in various business disputes as well as domestic squabbles. Lawyers and judges were known to say,

"Take this case to Twerski. You'll be able to avoid a costly and distressing trial."

This is not the place for a biography of my father. I tried to portray something of him in *Generation to Generation* and *Gevuros*. I will permit myself just one digression that best describes his dedication, wisdom, and emotional depth.

During World War II, one of the families in our synagogue received word that their son was missing in action in the European theater of war. Needless to say, the family was devastated, assuming the very worst. My father encouraged them never to abandon hope, that their son was a prisoner of war and would return one day. He used to visit the family every week to uphold their spirits.

After the war was over, the son did indeed return, having been a prisoner of war. When he returned to his home base, he found a stack of letters from my father, who had written to him every week. I am certain that my father wrote these letters prior to making his weekly visit to the family, to reinforce his own hope and faith that their son was alive, because his effort to keep the family's hopes high could be effective only if he believed in what he was telling them.

That is an important psychological insight. You cannot convince someone of something that you do not fully believe yourself.

Although I did not have my father's unique qualities, I nevertheless wanted to follow in his footsteps and provide counseling to people. However, my first few years as a rabbi held out little hope of achieving this.

After World War II, psychiatry and psychology had a meteoric rise, and it soon became apparent to me that people were not going to consult me for counseling, because they were going to go to a psychiatrist or psychologist. Pastoral counseling was still in its infancy. My function as a rabbi was going to be performing a variety of religious rituals: weddings, funerals, monument unveilings, and bar mitzvahs. The latter was particularly disappointing, because at that time, Jewish education in Milwaukee consisted of after-school classes, which the kids bitterly resented because they wanted to play football with their friends. Most parents had no intention of their children becoming religiously observant. The poor kids had to spend four years in after-school classes so that their parents could throw a party. I saw myself as an accomplice to a travesty of religion. I recall telling my wife that my bar mitzvah sermons were causing me intolerable nausea.

My decision to leave the rabbinate may also have been influenced by an episode that occurred when I visited a parishioner in the hospital who had undergone surgery. He said to me, "Your father was here yesterday. It was so remarkable, because ever since my operation, I was not free of pain. Nothing the doctors prescribed seemed to help. But yesterday, when your father walked in, I felt the pain lift off, as if by magic." I said to myself, *This is one act that I am not going to follow.*

Years earlier, I had harbored fantasies of becoming a physician, and as I became less and less enamored of being a rabbi, the medical profession became ever more inviting. One major obstacle was that medical school was then a six-day-a-week program, and whereas Orthodox Jewish law suspends Sabbath restrictions when there is a serious threat to health, that applies only to a doctor who is providing treatment for a patient, but not to a student in training. Imagine my surprise when I discovered that Marquette University's medical school had just switched to a five-day-a-week program. I took this as a providential sign that I was to become a physician. It appeared to me that G-d* indeed wanted me to be the kind of rabbi my father was. For this, I would have to obtain the imprimatur of psychia-

---

* It is customary in Orthodox Jewish practice not to write the name G-d or L-rd in full, in consideration of the fact that the page on which the name appears may someday be thrown away or destroyed, demonstrating disrespect for the Creator.

try, and the change in the medical school schedule now made this feasible.

At that time, the medical school had a quota. In a class of 102, they would admit only four Jews. I applied, as did a friend. I was accepted but he was not. He said, "Of course they accepted you. They are Jesuits, and you remind them of their savior."

The dean was concerned that my observance of Sabbath would conflict with my medical duties. I said, "Dr. Hirschboeck, I assure you that no patient will ever suffer from my Sabbath observance."

In the second year, the flunk-out course was pathology. I knew that there would be six days of Jewish holidays on which I could not attend classes. During summer vacation, I read the pathology text almost to the point of verbatim, and I received the highest score in the class even though I missed six lectures.

The first two years of medical school passed without incident, but in the third year a problem arose because all the lectures in pediatrics were on Saturday. This was long before the advent of digital voice recorders, so I asked a buddy to slip a sheet of carbon paper under his notes, and each Sunday I would get the lecture notes. I noticed that only the first one-third of the notes were legible, because thereafter my buddy was nodding off to sleep. The professor of pediatrics who gave the lecture was an excellent clinician who was without peer at the bedside, but terribly monotonous as a speaker. The notes were therefore of little help, but I would consult them to find out what subject was discussed in the lecture, and I would then read up on it in the textbook.

One day, I was summoned to the dean's office. "We do not take attendance, Twerski," Dr. Hirschboeck said, "but when you are not there, it is rather obvious." Since I was the only bearded student in the class, this was indeed true. I suggested to the dean that if my nonattendance at the Saturday lectures would result in unsatisfactory performance on the exam, he could dismiss me.

Lo and behold, when the exams were scored, I came in first in a class of one hundred. Why? Because my classmates relied on what they learned in the lectures, and inasmuch as most of them were somnolent at the lectures, the knowledge I had from reading the textbook far surpassed theirs.

I applied for an internship at Mt. Sinai Hospital in Milwaukee, where I was born, and I offered to work every Sunday in exchange for having Saturdays off. The staff did not grant me this, arguing that a doctor may attend to patients on the Sabbath. I did not enter into an argument with them, and I applied to St. Joseph's Hospital, where my request was promptly granted.

When the staff at Mt. Sinai got wind of this, they called my father. "Abe can't go to St. Joseph's," they said. "He belongs here."

"St. Joseph's respects his religion," my father said.

Mt. Sinai granted my request.

Having frequently visited Mt. Sinai as a rabbi and discussed patients with the doctors, I was a professional peer with them. Coming in as a far-junior subordinate was somewhat awkward, but a fortuitous incident greatly facilitated things for me. On the very first day of my internship, the highly respected chairman of the department of internal medicine invited me to make rounds with him. We entered a patient's room, and the doctor told me that this patient was being discharged. He was hospitalized for evaluation of persistent pain in his arms and legs, but the workup did not reveal a cause for this.

"That's easy," I said. "He has diabetic neuropathy" (a disease of the peripheral nerves occurring in diabetics).

"Why do you say that?" the doctor asked. "He's not diabetic," and he proceeded to show me that the patient's blood sugar level was perfectly normal.

"Why don't you run a five-hour glucose tolerance test on him?" I suggested. The doctor shrugged, but agreed to do so.

The following day, he confronted me. "Unbelievable," he said.

"You were right. He has a diabetic curve. What made you think of that?"

"Simple," I said. "This patient's father was my Hebrew tutor, and whenever my mother offered him coffee, he refused sugar and cookies, saying that he was diabetic. The patient might not even have known that his father was diabetic, but given that fact and the unexplained symptoms, I thought it was a likely diagnosis."

The story went around the hospital, and my reputation was made.

2
BREAKING THE CHAIN

Although I was disillusioned about the rabbinate, the decision to become a doctor did not come lightly. We have a family tree going back many generations, and there was a long chain of rabbis. If I became a doctor, I would break that chain, and that was an awesome responsibility.

For some time, I had a correspondence with Rabbi Yaakov Yisrael Kanievsky in Israel, who was considered the foremost Torah authority in the Jewish world. He and my father had been childhood friends in a village in the Ukraine where they lived. Only someone of his stature could approve of my breaking the chain, and I consulted him, fully expecting that he would tell me to keep the tradition. I was pleasantly surprised when he approved of my going to medical school.

However, the rabbi expressed concern. I was going to leave the world of Torah study for the world of secular science. I was going to be exposed to philosophies that were at odds with Jewish thought. I was going to learn all about evolution, which contradicted the sacred belief in Creation. The rabbi, therefore, suggested a number of safeguards to prevent me from deviating from Torah principles. Among these were to study Torah daily, to honor the holiness of the Sabbath by not studying any secular subjects or even reading a newspaper on the Sabbath, and to pray fervently for Divine guidance to not be swayed from the truth.

I followed the rabbi's suggestions, but his concern was really groundless. No one in college took the philosophy courses seriously. It was a more of a thought game, and a course where one could easily get an A. Insofar as evolution was concerned, the more I learned about science, and particularly about the intricacies of the human body and its function, the more I realized that the theory that this could have come about without direction of an omniscient and omnipotent G-d was absurd. I appreciated the words of the great twelfth-century philosopher and lawgiver, Rabbi Moses Maimonides, that the way one could achieve the adoration and awe of G-d was to study His great works of Creation.

In our daily prayers we thank G-d for "His kindnesses and miracles that are always with us." What are the constant miracles? We don't witness supernatural events every day. But as I came to realize the exquisite way in which the human body functions, I understood the constant miracles.

A physician who specializes in infertility problems told me, "One day I was peering through a microscope at a fertilized ovum, and I realized that henceforth, all that this cell will have is carbon, oxygen, hydrogen, nitrogen, and a few trace metals, and from them this single cell will develop into a whole human being, with a brain comprised of two hundred billion specialized cells. I knew at that moment that there must be a G-d."

So, far from causing me to lose faith in G-d, my scientific education strengthened it immensely.

3

THE LEBANESE RESCUER

During medical school, I was able to function as assistant rabbi in my father's congregation, and I received a small salary. Some members of the congregation helped out, as did my father to the best of his ability. I had three children, and I fell behind in tuition for two trimesters.

One day during lunch period, I called home, and my wife said, "What would you do if you had four thousand dollars?"

"We'd take a trip around the world," I said. "But I'm too busy to daydream now."

My wife said, "Well, you've got four thousand dollars."

"Where from?" I asked.

"From Danny Thomas," she said.

"Who is Danny Thomas?" I asked.

"From the television show," she said.

"Did you get a ticket to his quiz show?" I asked.

"No," she said, "Danny Thomas the comedian. Listen to this article in yesterday's *Chicago Sun*." Here's what she read to me:

"In a meeting with officials of Marquette University Medical School, the TV star Danny Thomas was told about a young rabbi who was having difficulty with his tuition. 'How much does your rabbi need?' Danny Thomas asked. 'About four thousand dollars,' the Marquette people said. 'Tell the rabbi he's got it,' Danny Thomas said."

Danny Thomas with Dr. Rabbi Twerski

The next day I received a special-delivery letter from Danny Thomas, apologizing for the account getting into the news, and asking me to forgive him if it caused me any embarrassment. Within the next two weeks, checks for four thousand dollars arrived.

One of the hospitals to which I applied for internship was Cedars of Lebanon in Los Angeles, and while there for an interview, I went to meet Danny Thomas at the studio in Hollywood.

Danny again apologized for the story getting into the media.

"Danny," I said, "the newspapers regularly report all the horrible things that happen in the world. Why should the good deeds be kept secret?"

"For us entertainers, publicity is our bread and butter. I did not want this to be a publicity stunt," Danny said.

The following year, Danny Thomas made a national tour to raise money for the Shrine of St. Jude, a hospital and research center that he sponsored, for the treatment of leukemia in children. One of the cities he visited was Milwaukee. I did a little fund-raising of my own, and at the banquet fund-raiser for the Shrine of St. Jude, I presented Danny with a check. I also gave him a silver-covered Bible, and I read the dedication from the prophet Micha (6:8): "O man, what is good and what does G-d seek from you: only the performance of justice, the love of kindness, and walking humbly with your G-d." Danny and I embraced, and there was not a dry eye in the audience.

So, the career of an Orthodox rabbi was saved by a Lebanese Christian. Only in America.

4
MEDICAL INTERNSHIP

Several interesting incidents occurred during my year of internship.

A Roman Catholic priest was admitted to the surgical service. He had been under treatment for aches and pains by a ninety-year-old physician who had lost his ability to practice medicine but had not lost his license. He had treated this patient with vitamins without having performed an adequate examination. When this elderly physician died, the patient consulted another physician, whose examination revealed a huge abdominal mass. He was admitted to the hospital for evaluation.

X-rays revealed that this huge mass was located behind the kidneys on the posterior abdominal wall. There was every reason to believe that this was a malignant tumor, which of course bode poorly for the priest's survival. Inasmuch as the exact nature of the mass could not be determined by laboratory tests, surgery was necessary, if only for the purpose of obtaining tissue for examination.

I assisted at the surgery, and the mass was found to be firmly affixed to the abdominal wall. Removal of the mass would be impossible. However, when the surgeon cut into the mass to get a piece of tissue for microscopic examination, some pus began to exude. He promptly put a suction tube into the mass, and after more than a liter of pus was drained, the mass collapsed. It was not a tumor after all, just a huge abscess. A cry of triumph went up in the operating room. Instead of cancer, it was an infection that could be treated successfully.

We were therefore quite disappointed when the priest did not respond well to treatment, but became weaker every day, refusing to eat or participate in postoperative exercises. It struck me that during his entire hospitalization, this man had not had a single visitor.

I called the local bishop, who told me that this priest had come to the United States after World War II and did not have a parish of his own. He would assist at different churches, wherever help was needed. Since he had no place where he appeared regularly, no one had noted his absence. The bishop assured me that he would notify people of the priest's illness, and on that very same day visitors began coming, some bringing flowers or boxes of candy. Very soon, the patient's spirits picked up, and within two weeks he left the hospital having made an excellent recovery.

At this point I had not had any formal training in psychiatry, but I learned in a very emphatic way that a human being is more than a mass of protoplasm and that emotional factors may be as important in treatment of illness as potent antibiotics.

A second incident was that of a patient who had been admitted to the hospital because of a fractured hip. During the surgery, he suffered a cardiac arrest. The surgeon promptly opened his chest, and by massaging his heart, restored its function.

Those were the days before IV nurses teams were in existence, and all intravenous medications had to be administered by a physician. I was called to administer an intravenous antibiotic, and when I inquired about the patient's condition, I was told about what had transpired during surgery. The nurse in attendance told me that the patient was not doing well at all. He was very depressed, did not eat, and would not even sit up in bed.

After I injected the antibiotic, the patient asked, "Doctor, are you also a rabbi?"

"Yes," I replied.

"I am not Jewish," he said. "I'm Catholic. Do you think you could pray with me?"

"Of course," I answered. Then I thought a bit about which prayers we might both have in common. "Let's say the twenty-third psalm," I said.

Together we began, "The L-rd is my shepherd, I shall not want." When we came to the verse, "Yea, though I walk through the valley of the shadow of death, I will fear no evil, for You are with me," the patient began to cry.

On the following day, I returned to see the patient, and the nurse told me that there had been a remarkable change in his demeanor. He was sitting up in bed, smiling, and eating with a voracious appetite. He greeted me with a broad grin. "Hi, doc," he said.

The patient then told me that when he emerged from the anesthesia, he found himself in the intensive care unit with his chest bandaged. He was informed of what had happened to his heart during surgery.

"I realized that I was vulnerable to another cardiac arrest at any time, but the next one might occur when there is no one around to get my heart going again. I was terrified of sudden death. I was not ready to die yet.

"When we said that prayer, I began to think differently. I am a retired police sergeant. I believe I discharged my duties faithfully and properly. During all those years on the police force I did enough good to expect that G-d will be with me.

"When we said, 'Though I walk through the valley of the shadow of death You are with me,' I knew that was written for me. How many people have had their heart stop and were in the valley of the shadow of death like I was? But now I realize that G-d is with me, and it is no longer frightening.

"I am now sixty-eight. If I do not get another cardiac arrest, I might live another ten years. If it should happen again, I might die tomorrow. Either way, I will not be alone, because G-d is with me."

Then he added, "The prayer sure beats the antibiotic any day."

The third incident was one which had a very significant impact on me and contributed a great deal to my understanding of human psychology and the marvelous workings of the mind. A fifty-year-old woman was admitted to the hospital for exploratory surgery because of a suspected tumor. She told the doctor that she was very active in community affairs and had assumed many important responsibilities. She stated that she was aware that a tumor might mean cancer, and that it was important for her to know the truth, since it would be unfair to many people and many organizations for her to continue carrying responsibilities if her health and ability to function were going to deteriorate. The doctor promised to be frank with her and reveal all the findings of the surgery.

In surgery it was found that she indeed had a cancerous tumor, which was removed, but because there was indication that the cancer had already spread, she would have to undergo a course of chemotherapy. She expressed her gratitude to the doctor for being truthful with her and said that she would cooperate in whatever treatment was recommended. She spoke freely with the nurses and the staff about her having cancer.

The administration of chemotherapy required intravenous injection, but this was difficult because she had poor veins. Each time she received chemotherapy, multiple attempts to find a vein were necessary. On one occasion, I was called to administer the medication, and as luck would have it, I found a vein on my first try. The patient concluded that I had some unique skill in giving intravenous medication, and requested that I be the one to administer all her medications.

The patient returned weekly for her chemotherapy. She would announce, "I'm here for my cancer shot." She remarked how fortunate she was to be living in an era when science had found a successful treatment for cancer, She appeared to be adjusting well, both physically and emotionally.

Several months after the surgery, she began experiencing joint pains and shortness of breath. The chemotherapy was no longer effective, and she was readmitted to the hospital. She was very angry and said, "I can't understand what it is with you doctors. I've been coming here regularly, and you just haven't been able to discover what's wrong with me."

The latter remark was astonishing to me, since she had repeatedly referred to her having cancer. It became evident that as long as cancer was something abstract and did not pose an immediate threat to her life, she could accept the diagnosis. Once the condition progressed to the point of causing pain and shortness of breath, concrete evidence that she was deteriorating, this was so threatening to her that her psychological system shut off the realization of the truth. She was not intentionally lying or pretending. At this time, she actually did not believe that she had cancer.

This is what *denial* is. Just as a person may faint from severe sudden pain, which is the body's way of providing relief from the perception of pain, so does the psychological system provide for unconscious rejection of a perception which is too threatening for a person to accept.

When I subsequently became involved in the treatment of alcoholism and drug addiction, where denial of the problem is prominent both for the chemically dependent person and for members of the family, the awareness of denial that I gathered from this woman's case was extremely helpful. People who observe the alcoholic, drug addict, or their family members are often bewildered by how they can all overlook something which is so blatantly obvious. They tend to think that these people are willfully concealing facts or putting on an act. Alcoholics and addicts do lie, but sometimes it is more than lying. The defense of denial may cause a person to be totally oblivious to something that is grossly evident to everyone else.

I applied to several psychiatric training programs, one of which was at Northwestern University in Chicago. I was interviewed by the head of the department, a renowned psychoanalyst. He expressed some concern that my Orthodox religion would limit my effectiveness as a psychiatrist. Inasmuch as he was convinced by Freud that religion was a neurosis, which meant that religious people should be treated to be free of all religious restraints, I did not think he would accept me.

Suddenly, we heard a thud. The coatrack outside his office had fallen over, and the coats on it fell to the floor. I helped him set the rack upright and put the coats back. The rack was leaning forward a bit, and the doctor said, "Let's turn it around so it leans toward the wall. That way, even if it falls, the wall will support it."

I said, "Doctor, that's the value of religion. Even if someone falls, there is something to support him."

I was accepted to his program, but for reasons I can't remember, I chose the University of Pittsburgh.

5
A HUMBLING EXPERIENCE

I MENTIONED EARLIER THAT I HAD had fantasies of becoming a doctor. I did not know what the origin of these fantasies were until much later, when I discovered I was really a power-hungry person, and that being a doctor was a very powerful position. It would give me control over life and death. In addition, it would solve my problem of low self-esteem. The people I cured would admire me. These are rather common drives, and are not really problematic unless they become intense.

Although I was now a physician, the hospitals still had me on their list of clergy. One night I received a call from a hospital where a woman requested to see a rabbi. I drove to the hospital and was directed to the nursery, where I met a distraught woman standing over a bassinet in which her newborn infant was struggling to survive. The baby had been born with what was then an inoperable heart defect and could not survive. The woman looked at me tearfully and said, "Why did G-d put me through a difficult pregnancy and allow me to look forward to having a child, and now I have to stand here and watch my baby die. Why, rabbi? Why?"

I stood there in utter silence. At first, I could not think of anything to say. Then I said, "Neither I nor anyone else can know why these things happen. But inasmuch as you believe in G-d, would you want to say a prayer?" She said that she would, and I prayed with her.

The next morning I told my father about the incident. I told him that I felt the woman's pain and could not help feeling angry at G-d for letting it happen. My father said, "Are you sure that you are identifying your feelings correctly? Are you really feeling the pain of the woman, or are you feeling your own distress over being helpless? Here you are, armed with the two greatest forces known to humanity, medicine and religion, and you are faced with a case of an infant who is going to die and a bereaved mother whom you could not comfort?"

I had to admit my father was right. My feelings were quite selfish. I did not want to admit that my feelings were more for myself than for the agonizing mother. I began to have some insight into the lust for power, and how threatening it is to feel powerless.

But the lust for power is not so easily overcome. During my tour of duty in the emergency room there were ample opportunities to feel powerful, especially when a patient was brought with an attack of acute asthma and was fighting for air. A quick injection of epinephrine and intravenous aminophylline, and he was breathing comfortably. "Thank you, doctor. You saved my life." That is enough to make one feel ten feet tall.

Or, consider someone admitted to the ER in insulin shock due to an overdose of insulin or an unusual reaction to the proper dose. The anxious family is afraid the patient will die, and the hero doctor administers an intravenous injection of 50 percent glucose. Instantaneously, the patient is alert and smiling, and the family sees the doctor as their savior. No wonder some doctors think they are G-d, and I was no exception.

There are things that can bring one down to reality. The psychiatric hospital where I received my training had locked wards. I was walking down the hall, jingling the keys in my pocket, when one patient said, "Doctor, you don't have to remind me that I am locked in here but that you have the key." That brought me down a notch.

I was humbled by a patient who taught me gratitude. I always thought of myself as being a grateful person. I appreciated what others did for me and I sincerely thanked them. But there was still something about gratitude that I had to learn.

I had just bought a new car, equipped with every extra. One feature it had that was especially valuable for me was cruise control. I have a tendency to speed, and I could be speeding without being aware of it. So I use cruise control. For me, it's like Antabuse for an alcoholic. Antabuse is a medication that makes you deathly ill if you drink, so it gives you the control you don't have.

Well, my cruise control was not accurate. I would set it at sixty miles an hour and it would vacillate between fifty-five and sixty-five. I could have it fine-tuned, but that would mean taking the car to the dealer, spending several hours waiting, and so on.

That day, a recovering alcoholic woman came for a follow-up visit. She had managed eight months of sobriety and was thankful that she had found a job. "I may be able to save enough money to get my car fixed," she said.

"What's wrong with your car?" I asked.

"It doesn't have a reverse gear," she said.

"How do you drive without a reverse gear?" I asked.

She said, "Oh, I can drive all right. I just have to be careful where I park. I have to remember that there are some people who don't have a car at all."

If I could have dug a deep hole in the ground, I would have jumped in. This woman was grateful that she had a car, albeit without a reverse gear, and here I was griping because my fully equipped new car had a cruise control that lacked precision.

One incident was not only humbling, but actually crushing. Caroline was a sixteen-year-old girl whom I inherited from the resident that had left the service. Her primary problem was that she refused to go to school. I had several senior psychiatrists as my supervisors, and the one for Caroline was a rather aggressive doctor. He told me, "The way I deal with such cases is that I drive them to school, then they go."

I followed my supervisor's instructions. I told Caroline, "Tomorrow morning I will drive by here at eight o'clock, and I expect you to be waiting at the hospital door." Sure enough, Caroline was there at eight, and I drove her to school. When she returned, I had an hourlong session with her, reviewing the day, and she seemed very pleased. The following morning, I again drove her to school.

Later that day, I was called to the office of the clinical director, who was my chief mentor. He said, "I understand that you've been driving Caroline to school."

"Yes, that's what Dr. R. told me to do," I said.

"Dr. R. is in private practice and he can do as he wishes," he said. "I am the director of an institution. I can trust you, Dr. Twerski, but there are thirty residents here, and I am not sure I can trust them all. I cannot let a resident take a young female patient in his car. You can explain that to Caroline."

I told Caroline why I could no longer drive her. Then I said, "You've seen that you did well at school these two days. I will be here tomorrow when you return from school and we'll discuss how the day went."

Later that morning, I was called to the clinical director's office. "We just received a call from the police. On the way to school, Caroline jumped off the bridge and killed herself."

I was numb with shock. Then the tears started flowing down my face. The chief said, "Abe, you did what was right, following the instructions of your supervisor. I did what was right by stopping you from driving her."

"But she's dead," I said, "and it's my fault. I shouldn't be in charge of people's lives."

"In your first year of training, you've learned what others may not learn for decades," the chief said. "You can do what is right and have a disastrous result. Every doctor has patients who die. If you leave psychiatry because you are unable to handle a patient's death, then that will leave only doctors who don't give a hoot about a patient's death. I'd rather have you as my doctor."

For the next few weeks the chief held my hand to make sure I was okay.

When a patient dies from heart disease, the doctor may be consoled by the fact that the available heart medications have their limitations. If a patient dies from pneumonia, the doctor is consoled that antibiotics have their limitations. The patient dies because the medications are just not good enough. As a psychiatrist, I, not the medication, am the treatment. If my patient committed suicide, it was I that was not good enough, and that is very, very humbling.

Caroline's suicide occurred in December 1960. Every December, even fifty-three years later, I experience an anniversary reaction.

6
MY MOTHER'S CONTRIBUTION

My mother certainly had a great influence on me, although it was more subtle than my father's. I was not aware of some of her contributions until later in life. One of the things she often repeated was the holy verse "Do not judge a person until you've been in his position" (*Ethics of the Fathers* 2:5). This has been a guiding principle throughout my life.

My mother used to tell me bedtime stories. She did not have a huge repertoire, so I heard the same stories many times. There was one story I did not think of until the following incident.

Once a young doctor consulted me. He was finishing his first year of radiology training and was not happy with this specialty. He said that prior to this he had one year of internal medicine, but he did not like that either. He was now trying to decide between psychiatry and pathology.

I became a bit suspicious. There can be no greater contrast between two specialties than psychiatry and pathology. One is entirely based on interpersonal relationships, and the other is totally devoid of any interpersonal relationships.

"Before medical school, did you train for anything else?" I asked him. He said that he had a year of engineering, but he did not like it.

"How come you stayed in medical school?"

"My father would have killed me if I dropped out," he said.

At that point, I remembered the story my mother had told me that I had not thought of in more than thirty years. It went like this:

ONCE THERE was a stonecutter who earned his living hewing slabs of stone from a mountain. He often bewailed his sorry fate. "I have to work from dawn to dusk, breaking my back lifting this heavy pickax all day," he cried, "and then I barely earn enough to put bread on the table for my family."

One day he heard a tumult. Climbing to the peak of the mountain, he could see from afar that there was a parade in the city. The king was in a royal procession, and people had lined the streets shouting "Bravo! Long live the king!" and throwing flowers at the royal coach.

The stonecutter raised his eyes to heaven. "Dear L-rd," he said, "You are a just G-d. That king and I are both human beings. Where is the justice that he should be so mighty and powerful, and I should be so downtrodden? If You are indeed just, You will give me the opportunity to be mighty as the king."

Suddenly, he felt himself transformed. G-d had answered his prayer. He was the mighty king, receiving the accolades from thousands of loyal subjects. How thrilling it was to be so powerful!

But then he began to feel very uncomfortable. Clad in

his ermine robe, he was wilting as the sun's rays fell upon him. "What?" he said. "The sun can humble a king? Then the sun is most powerful. I wish to be the sun."

He was transformed into the sun, and he enjoyed its unequaled power. But then he found himself frustrated. A dark cloud had passed beneath him and was not allowing his rays to penetrate.

"What?" he said. "A cloud can frustrate the sun? Then it must be more mighty than the sun. I wish to be a cloud."

As a cloud he took great pleasure in frustrating the sun, but then a sharp gust of wind blew him away. "The wind must be mightier than a cloud. I wish to be the wind."

As the wind, he became ferocious, causing tidal waves and leveling forests. But suddenly he was stymied. He had encountered a tall mountain, which resisted his strongest gusts. "If a mountain is mightier than the wind, I wish to be a tall mountain."

As a tall mountain he dwarfed all else on earth, and felt most powerful. But then he felt a sharp pain. A stonecutter wielding a pickax was tearing away parts of him. He said, "If a stonecutter can dismantle a mountain, then he must be even mightier than the mountain. I wish to be that stonecutter."

And so he became the mightiest of all: a stonecutter.

I HAD not thought of that story until this young man told me that he was dissatisfied with everything he had studied. I told him the story and said, "If you will be happy with yourself as a person, then you can be happy being an engineer or whatever kind of doctor you choose to be. If you are not happy with yourself, you can exhaust all the medical specialties and all the professions in the world, and you will remain dissatisfied."

When I was five years old, I could not appreciate the wisdom in this bedtime story. It became apparent to me only many years later.

A person with internal happiness can adjust to whatever position he attains. A person who seeks happiness in external sources may never be satisfied. He may be obstinate in making constant changes in the expectation of something that will relieve his discontent. Each change brings but a fleeting relief, and he may exhaust himself in a futile search for happiness.

Another story my mother told me was about a man who suffered extreme poverty. One day he prayed for a miracle that would make him rich. The next morning, when he awoke, he found a purse near his bed. When he opened it, he found a dollar bill, and when he removed the dollar bill, another one appeared in its place. He was overjoyed, and kept on pulling out dollar bills. Three days later, he was found dead, lying on a huge pile of dollar bills.

Only much later did I realize that my mother had taught me the prototype of addiction. The addict never has enough of a drug, and keeps on increasing his use of it until it kills him.

I used to take my children to my mother to hear her stories. They loved to listen to her. I regret that I did not stay to listen to them. I might have become much wiser.

7
THE NUCLEUS WITHIN

I WAS IN MY SECOND YEAR of psychiatric training when I received a call from the psych emergency room. A woman said she had to see a psychiatrist promptly and could not wait for an appointment.

Isabel was sixty-one. She was one of three daughters of an Episcopalian priest. Isabel began drinking late in adolescence, and at twenty she was into very heavy drinking. She married and had a child. When the child was three, her husband said, "Make your choice. It's either the booze or the family."

"I knew I could not stop drinking," Isabel said, "and I wasn't much of a wife or mother. It was only decent to give him the divorce he asked for."

At sixty-one, Isabel was attractive, and she must have been stunning at twenty-eight. Through her social contacts, she acquired a beautiful apartment, the latest in fashion, and all the alcohol she wanted. The vast amounts of alcohol she drank caused her life to deteriorate, and after five years, she was living in run-down hotels and barely surviving.

Every so often, Isabel was found unconscious and taken to a hospital for detoxification. She attended an AA meeting in the hospital, and upon discharge promptly resumed drinking. When I assumed the position as director of psychiatry at St. Francis Hospital, I looked up Isabel's record. Between 1938 and 1956, Isabel had been detoxed at this hospital fifty-nine times. At another hospital that offered detox she had twenty-two admissions. I was unable to get any information from other hospitals where she had undergone detoxification.

Isabel's family was horrified by her behavior and disowned her. Her sisters answered her phone calls with a brusque "Don't you dare call me again" and then hung up.

In 1956, Isabel approached a lawyer who had helped her out of some alcohol-related jams. "David, I need a favor," she said.

"Good heavens," the lawyer said. "Not again. What did you do this time?"

"I'm not in any trouble," Isabel said. "I want you to put me away in the state hospital for a year."

At that time Pennsylvania statutes had an Inebriate Act, under which a chronic alcoholic could be committed to a state hospital for "a year and one day." This law had been used by families who wanted to get a chronic alcoholic out of their hair. No alcoholic had ever asked to be put away for a year.

"You don't know what you're asking for," the lawyer said. "You're crazy."

"If I'm crazy, I really belong in the state hospital," Isabel said.

Isabel continued to press her request, and the lawyer finally took her before the judge and had her committed to the state hospital.

After a year of sobriety, Isabel left the state hospital and promptly went to an AA meeting. Someone gave her a few nights of shelter, and she soon found a job as a housekeeper for a nationally renowned physician.

The doctor was retired and was a chronic alcoholic. Many

times Isabel had to lift him off the floor and put him in bed. He sat on the board of several foundations and was periodically called to testify at Senate hearings. Isabel would receive a call from the doctor's children. "Dad has to be in Washington in two weeks," they'd tell her. "Get him into shape." Isabel would detox the doctor, get him a haircut and shave, and put him on the plane to Washington.

"Now don't you drink on the plane or in Washington," she would say. "When you come back tomorrow, I'll be waiting for you with a bottle." The doctor obeyed like a well-trained puppy.

I had never heard anything like this before. My first career was as a rabbi, and seminary did not teach me anything about alcoholism. Medical school was no better. I learned much about some rare diseases but nothing about the most common disease a doctor encounters. In my psychiatric training I was learning much about mental illnesses, but alcohol and drugs were never mentioned.

I was so fascinated by Isabel's story that I neglected to ask her what the acute emergency was. As a fledgling psychiatrist, I knew that there had to be a motivation for a person to seek help. What could possibly have motivated Isabel to take so drastic a measure as to commit herself to a state mental hospital for a year by court order? I had to discover her reason, so I told her to come back the next week for another session.

In the following session I heard some more interesting stories. Inasmuch as I did not have a clue about her motivation, I had her come back the next week. To make a long story short, I saw Isabel once a week for thirteen years. One night, at age seventy-four, she died peacefully in her sleep.

Back to the story, I was curious as to how she was managing to stay sober. It was obvious to me that medicine and psychiatry had no effective treatment for alcoholism. What was her secret?

"I go to meetings of Alcoholics Anonymous," she said. In 1961, none of the celebrities had revealed that they were recovering alcoholics. Few people outside of AA knew anything about it.

"What happens at these meetings?" I asked. "Who provides the treatment?"

"We have speakers' meetings and discussion meetings, and we share our experiences," Isabel said.

"Do you have psychiatrists or psychologists there?" I asked.

"There is one psychologist who shows up occasionally, but he's still drunk most of the time."

"Look, Isabel," I said, "some kind of treatment must be going on at these meetings if they are keeping you sober. Can I come and see for myself?"

"Sure," Isabel said. That week she took me to my first AA meeting.

The first thing that struck me at the meeting was that there was no stratification. Everyone was equal. No one could become president of the organization, and furthermore, money could not buy any special privileges.

As a rabbi, part of my job was to raise funds to cover my congregation's annual budget. Money came from the congregants' donations. People of lesser means made smaller contributions, and wealthier people made substantial contributions. I liked everyone equally, but I had to handle the large donors with silk gloves. I could not risk offending them, lest they leave for another congregation. Wealthy congregants received special treatment.

It is said that before G-d, everyone is equal. G-d can afford to treat everyone equally. He doesn't have to make mortgage payments each month. I did.

Any organization that is dependent on contributions is in the same situation. People with money or political clout are given preferential treatment. What impressed me about AA was that once people entered the room, everyone was equal. The rich received no special attention. Sometimes a poor person was in the position to help a wealthy person. Nor did academic status count. A fifth-grade dropout and a PhD were treated equally. I had never encountered anything like this.

Here is an example of AA's independence. I received a call from a man who said that he wanted to make a contribution of ten thousand dollars to AA in memory of his late sister, who had enjoyed fourteen years of sobriety with the help of AA. He asked me where to send the check.

I called several people in AA, and when no one could help me, I called the AA central office. "Don't send the check here," they said. "We can't do anything with it."

"Then how can this man make a contribution?" I asked.

"He can cash the check at the bank and go to a meeting. When they pass the basket, he can put the money in."

"You want him to put ten thousand dollars in cash in the basket?" I asked.

"Yes," was the answer. "But if he's not in the program, they might return it to him."

Never before and never since have I come across an organization that refuses donations.

My fascination with AA brought me back to more meetings. As I became familiar with the twelve steps for recovery, I concluded that they were a formula for mature, responsible living. There was nothing unique about alcoholics that made the twelve steps specifically for them. I found that virtually every character defect that can be found in alcoholics can also be found in nonalcoholics, albeit they may be less pronounced. The twelve steps were a way for proper living, and I could apply them to myself.

So began my involvement with AA. I have attended meetings in many cities in the United States and in many countries I have visited. I can find friends in a community where I do not know a single person.

What about the secret of Isabel's motivation to put herself into a state hospital? I never did solve that mystery in the thirteen years of therapy. I was left to my own devices to guess at it, and here is what I think.

Do you know how a volcano is formed? Deep down at the core of the earth, there is melted rock that is under extreme pressure. Over many centuries, this lava slowly makes its way through fissures in the earth's crust to the surface. Once it breaks through the surface, the lava erupts.

I believe that at the core of every human being there is a nucleus of self-respect and dignity. For a variety of reasons, this nucleus may be concealed and suppressed. Like the lava, it seeks to break through the surface and be recognized. Once it breaks through into a person's awareness, one may feel, "I am too good to be acting this way. This behavior is beneath my dignity." I think this is the "spiritual awakening" to which the twelfth step refers.

I think that this is what happened to Isabel. For years she had been blind to her self-worth and saw nothing wrong with her alcoholic behavior. Then one day, the nucleus of self-respect that had been buried deep within her broke through the surface, and she realized that she had no right to demean herself.

We have no right to be anything less than we can be.

8

ST. FRANCIS GENERAL HOSPITAL

Part of my three-year psychiatric training program required spending two months at the psychiatric unit of St. Francis General Hospital in Pittsburgh, which was run by the Sisters of St. Francis.

St. Francis Hospital was unique in that of its 750 beds, three hundred were psychiatric. The psychiatric unit was the only emergency service in the tristate area (Pennsylvania, Ohio, and West Virginia). The unit had an alcoholism treatment ward with an open admission policy. Any intoxicated person could be admitted and could leave at will. One alcoholic was admitted thirty-one times in a single month.

In order to support my family during my residency training, I entered an agreement with the Commonwealth of Pennsylvania to serve for two years on the staff of a state hospital, and in turn, they would increase my stipend.

The head of the department of psychiatry at the university, Dr. Henry Brosin, took a liking to me, and assured me that upon completing my term at the state hospital, I would join the teaching staff at the university. When I completed my term at the state hospital, I met with Dr. Brosin.

"Abe," he said, "you're welcome to join the staff, but I have a favor to ask of you. You know that St. Francis Hospital has been the primary resource for acute psychiatric treatment in Pittsburgh, and we owe them a huge debt of gratitude. St. Francis has not been able to hold onto a director of their psychiatric department. I think you could do the job, and I'm asking you to consider it."

I was stunned, and I just sat there in silence. "You think I'm *meshuga* (crazy)," Dr. Brosin said.

"You said it. I didn't," I responded.

"Look," Dr. Brosin said. "Meet with Sister Adele, the hospital administrator. Give it a trial for a year. You can always come back to our staff."

I had no intention of taking the position at St. Francis, but to please the boss, I met with Sister Adele. She was an extraordinary person (I will be disappointed if the Catholic Church does not canonize her), and I was impressed by her devotion to patient care. I looked for some way to refuse her without offending her.

"Sister," I said, "I worked here for two months. There are many psychiatric emergencies, and you need someone who is available 24/7/365. At sundown Friday, my telephone is shut down for twenty-six hours, and I can't be reached."

"Dr. Twerski," Sister said, "we would never think of calling you on your Sabbath."

That didn't work, so I said, "Sister, this is June, and I am taking my family to Israel for two months. I won't be available until October."

"We've waited this long, and we can wait a few more months," Sister said.

"Let me think it over," I said. Sister escorted me to the door. "Dr. Twerski," she said, "I know you are going to be our director of psychiatry. Our savior sent you to us."

After discussing it with my wife, I decided to give it a try for one year. That ended up being twenty years, during which I revolutionized the psychiatric department, but that's not the focus of this book. I just wanted you to know how I ended up at St. Francis.

There were no inviolable rules at St. Francis, except for one: no one in need of help could be turned away. Every morning, Sister Adele would review the emergency room log for the previous night, and if it appeared to her that a person who needed help was turned away, she would delay all other hospital business until this was clarified to her satisfaction.

I would sometimes leave the hospital at the end of the day with three patients being held overnight in the emergency room because there were no vacancies for admission. When I arrived the next morning, not only had those three been admitted, but three additional patients were admitted as well, although there had not been any discharges. I was never able to figure that out.

In past years, patients who were seriously mentally ill could be admitted to a hospital and treated without their consent if a licensed physician attested that their condition warranted this. As a result of the exposé that Communist Russia was incarcerating political dissidents in psychiatric hospitals, laws were passed in a number of states that prohibited hospitalizing a person without procedural due process. Although this legislation was intended to prevent abuses, this aspect of guaranteeing civil liberties had its drawbacks, because the result was that a large number of homeless people who could not care for themselves and found food and shelter in mental hospitals were now roaming the streets, exposed to the elements and scavenging garbage cans in search of food.

One such person was an elderly woman who was brought to the hospital by Travelers Aid on a cold winter night. She had been riding in buses to keep warm. According to the law, a hearing was held to determine whether she could be held in the hospital. The attorney appointed by the county to defend her civil liberties found a technicality to dismiss the case. He then asked me,

"What are you going to do with her?"

"I have no choice," I said. "I'll discharge her."

"But she'll die on the streets," he said.

"It was you who got her released," I replied.

"That's my job," he said.

Under the new legislation, involuntary admission for mental illness could occur only if there was "clear and present danger to life or health," which for practical purposes meant either a suicidal or homicidal threat. Furthermore, a physician's opinion did not suffice. The physician had to call a "mental health official," who was a lay person with little or no training in psychology or psychiatry, and describe the behavior that warranted hospitalization. If this "mental health official" felt that the behavior did not constitute "clear and present danger," the patient could not be hospitalized.

This situation caused Sister Adele indescribable agony. She envisioned, and correctly so, that the result of these regulations would be that people in desperate need of treatment were deprived of it. This was the subject of several meetings during which she poured her heart out to me, looking for solutions to the problem.

On numerous occasions, I received a call in the early morning hours. Sister Adele was in the emergency room with a distraught family, one member of which was refusing admission, and it was evident to her that he/she needed help, yet the law precluded involuntary admission. "What can we do, doctor?" Sister would say. "This person needs help."

"Sister, if you are willing to go to jail along with me, we will disregard the law and admit the patient," I would say.

I am certain that a number of suicides and other disasters were averted because Sister elected to do what she knew was right, although she was placing herself and the hospital in legal jeopardy.

Sister Adele was uncompromising in her religious convictions, and when pressure was put on the hospital to do things that she saw as possibly violating church law, she was tormented. There was never any consideration of compromise. If there was indeed a conflict, she would not yield even if it meant relinquishing administration of the hospital that the Sisters of St. Francis had founded. However, since the issues were not always clear, she could not come to a definite decision, and on such occasions she would call me for consultation.

Ultimately, the particular question would have to be submitted to the church authorities, but her discussions with me were to clarify the issues for herself and to enable her to present them to the authorities in a clear and concise manner. Sister respected my Orthodoxy and knew that, by the same token, I respected her beliefs and would assist her in formulating the questions.

An example of this was a request from the staff obstetricians for permission to perform tubal ligations to prevent pregnancy. There was no question in Sister's mind that sterilization for birth control could not be condoned. However, there might be cases where the woman's health might render this procedure permissible. Among health considerations would be the emotional state of a woman for whom a pregnancy might be an overwhelming stress and a danger to her mental health. But since the evaluation of an emotional state cannot be confirmed by objective laboratory data or indisputable physical findings, Sister was concerned that a woman desiring sterilization for birth control might feign emotional illness.

The issue was submitted to the local church authorities, who recommended a case-by-case evaluation by a panel of physicians, one of whom must be a psychiatrist. For Sister, this was not yet adequate assurance, and she acquiesced to this decision only if I would be the psychiatrist involved in the evaluation. For the duration of Sister's tenure as administrator of the hospital, all requests for tubal ligation on the basis of mental health required my approval.

In the late 1960s, the federal government allotted funds for the development of community mental health centers to make psychiatric services more accessible to those in need, and it was ready to dispense funds quite lavishly. The regulations required that a mental health center serve a designated "catchment area," encompassing a population of not over two hundred thousand. While Sister saw this as an opportunity to help more people with an expanded staff, she was very concerned about limiting services to a specific area. Her feeling was that help must be provided according to need and that where someone lived should not determine eligibility for help.

I assured Sister that the hospital could continue to provide services to everyone as it had done in the past, and the area restrictions would apply only to those new services that we would establish under the government grant. We would not be compelled to deny services to anyone.

Sister was not reassured. Restrictions are restrictions, and sooner or later, tight boundaries would be drawn and the inexorable fiat of the bureaucracy would direct people where to go, much as had happened with school districting. Time proved Sister to have been right.

Nevertheless, I sincerely believed that the federal grant would increase our capacity to provide services, and I did not share Sister's anxiety. However, Sister was most reluctant to apply for the federal grant, constantly reiterating her fear that "they will make us send away people who need help."

One day I said to Sister that since we were unable to come to a decision about what the correct thing to do is, we should pray for Divine enlightenment. Several days later, I told her that I had been praying, and that inasmuch as it appeared to me that the proper thing to do was to develop the mental health center, this must be the Divine will.

Without a moment's hesitation, Sister signed the application, thereby bringing to Pittsburgh its first, largest, and most efficient comprehensive mental health center.

9
MEETING THE BISHOP

In 1965, I assumed the position as director of the department of psychiatry at St. Francis. Several months after I joined the hospital, I received a call from Sister Adele. "The bishop wants to meet with you. I'll have the hospital driver take you there."

Bishop Wright was a very bright and assertive person. He was witty and loved to tell jokes. He could laugh so hard as to make the walls shake. Although I had never met him before, he greeted me with a huge bear hug. "I've heard many good things about you, rabbi," he said. (The bishop always referred to me as rabbi, not doctor.) "We're glad to have you at St. Francis." I thanked him for the compliment.

"We have a problem you can help us with," the bishop said. "As you know, Vatican II has made some major changes in the church. Some of these affect the convents, such as permission to change to civilian clothes rather than the traditional habit, and permission to go out unaccompanied by another nun. Whereas heretofore sisters' occupations had been essentially restricted to hospital work or school teaching, they will now be permitted a wide choice of careers."

There were also organizational changes within the convent. For example, when I came to St. Francis Hospital, Sister Adele introduced me to Mother Viola, a very pleasant woman who was said to rule the order with an iron fist. Under the new regulations, the title "Mother" was replaced with the more democratic "Sister." (I insisted on calling her "Mother Viola," and indeed, every Mother's Day I would send her a Mother's Day card, which she enjoyed immensely.)

Some of the sisters were having problems adjusting to these new rules. Apparently many nuns were not adapting well to the liberal changes and were showing signs of emotional stress. Some were leaving the religious community.

"I can't send them to the secular psychiatrists," the bishop said, "because they are likely to attack their religion and blame all their problems on their deprivations due to their vows of chastity, obedience, and poverty. I don't know why they don't realize that all of the patients they are treating do not have these restrictions, yet they are prone to incriminate the vows as causing the sisters' problems. I know that I can trust you to help the sisters."

I said, "I am flattered, bishop, but I am already working twenty-six hours a day. There's no way I can take on treatment of the sisters."

"I didn't mean that you have to do it yourself," the bishop said. "If you handpick a staff and they will be under your supervision, I will feel comfortable with that. The diocese will underwrite all the costs."

I said, "There's one problem, bishop. Sometimes a person distorts religion as an expression of his emotional difficulties. I have no way of knowing which religious behavior is normal and which is a distortion."

"I understand," the bishop said. "I will assign a priest who you may consult."

I said to the bishop, "There may be some nuns who entered

religious life as an escape from emotional distress. If they are treated, they may leave the convent."

"We don't want nuns who use religion to relieve their anxiety," the bishop said.

"What would happen if there was a mass exodus?" I asked.

The bishop laughed. "The church will survive, rabbi," he said. "If it has been able to survive in spite of its bishops, it can survive anything."

At this point I could not contain myself. "You know, bishop," I said, "the historical relationship between the church and the Jews has not always been pleasant. Isn't it a bit ironic that when the church is in trouble, you have recourse to a rabbi?"

The bishop smiled. "My dear rabbi," he said, "even in the worst of times, the popes' personal physicians were Jewish."

"Well, then, "I said, "if you should make it to the papacy, you already have your personal Jewish doctor. The only problem is that you chose a psychiatrist, and that might cause some people to raise their eyebrows." The bishop responded with a hearty laugh and a bear hug that almost crushed my ribs.

I told the bishop that I would do my best to organize this project. As I was about to leave, he bowed his head. "Bless me, rabbi," he said. Every time we met, that is how I took leave of him.

I proceeded to hire several psychiatrists and psychologists. The bishop appointed Father Moylan as our religious adviser. The word went out to all the convents and seminaries that anyone with a psychological problem should contact Father Moylan, who would refer the person to one of our group. The team met once a week to discuss cases. This service continued for about five years, until the nuns adjusted to the changes introduced by Vatican II and things settled down.

10

THE CARDINAL'S ASPIRATIONS

AFTER THE BISHOP WAS ELEVATED to cardinal and moved to Rome, he visited Pittsburgh once a year, and I would meet with him on these occasions. On one such visit, I met him in his quarters and I noticed that he was sitting very rigidly, hardly moving.

"Are you okay, cardinal?" I asked.

"Is it obvious?" he said. "I am in agony. I slipped on the floor getting out of bed and I hurt my back."

"You may have fractured a vertebra," I said. "You must have it X-rayed."

"You think so?" the cardinal said. "Then I must go to Mercy Hospital for the X-ray."

I said, "No way. Not with me around. You are going to St. Francis." I called ahead and notified the hospital that I was bringing the cardinal, and to admit him promptly with no red tape.

The cardinal was at that time being visited by a bishop, and I drove them to St. Francis Hospital. I don't think I ever drove as cautiously as I did then. I wanted to avoid a sudden stop that might give the cardinal a jolt.

On the way, the cardinal and the bishop exchanged some funny stories about the church, and the cardinal laughed so hard that it caused back pain. "Rabbi," he said, "if you can't be humorous about your own religion, you are in trouble."

The X-ray did indeed reveal a vertebral fracture. The cardinal was hospitalized for several days, and I visited him daily. When we were alone in his room, he said, "Rabbi, I don't know if the doctors are being honest with me. I have a muscle-wasting disease. To stand up from a sitting position, I must lift myself with my hands. I need to know how progressive this disease is. I have many responsibilities in the church, and I need to know how ambulatory I will be. Please look at my chart and tell me the truth."

"Why are you worried about being ambulatory?" I said. "From the pictures I've seen, you get carried on a chair."

The cardinal laughed. He wanted to become pope in the worst way. He saw the movie *The Shoes of the Fisherman* four times. He said, "You know, rabbi, there has been a pattern in the papacy, with fat popes and thin popes alternating, and Pope Paul is thin." (Cardinal Wright was quite heavy.)

I was frank with the cardinal and told him that eventually he would not be able to ambulate and would probably need a wheelchair. He thanked me, then lowered his head. "Bless me, rabbi," he said.

11
THE POPE'S MITZVAH

MY SERVICE TO THE DIOCESE INCLUDED priests and monks as well as nuns.

A thirty-four-year-old priest was admitted for alcoholism. He had been a very heavy drinker, and in the evening, the nurse on the alcoholism unit called to tell me that he was complaining that we have his parents trapped in the elevator shaft. I realized that he was having a serious withdrawal reaction and was hallucinating. I had him transferred to the intensive care unit. He went into *delerium tremens,* a severe withdrawal reaction that can be fatal. He spent five days in the intensive care unit during which his heart rate was above two hundred beats per minute, and he was given the last rites.

After he stabilized, I kept him in the general hospital rather than on the alcoholism unit because I was afraid that he might still be in withdrawal. When I visited him, the nurse told me that he had requested mouthwash several times. Mouthwash contains alcohol. When I confronted him, he denied drinking it. When I told him I was calling a lab technician to do a blood alcohol level, he admitted drinking the mouthwash.

"Father, you almost died from alcoholism," I said. "You were given the last rites because we did not think you would survive. If, after that, you can drink mouthwash, you have absolutely no control. In order for you to live, you must take Antabuse." Antabuse is a drug that prevents a person from drinking, because even a drop of alcohol precipitates a very repulsive reaction.

"Can I conduct the mass?" Father asked. "I must take a sip of wine."

I said, "No, you cannot take even a single sip of wine. You can use grape juice for the mass."

Father said, "No, it can't be grape juice. It must be wine."

"Let me see what I can do about that," I said. I called the local bishop, who was unable to help me because there was no provision for use of grape juice in the mass.

By this time, Bishop Wright had been promoted to cardinal and was in the Vatican. I called him in the Vatican and said, "Cardinal, you must help me save this priest's life. Please get him a dispensation to use grape juice instead of wine in the mass."

"Rabbi," the cardinal said, "I will personally hand-carry it to the holy father (Pope Paul VI)." The next day, the cardinal called, saying that the Pope had issued a dispensation for all priests who were alcoholics that they may use grape juice instead of wine in the mass.

"Thank you, cardinal," I said. "Tell the pope he did a mitzvah (virtuous deed)."

12

OBEDIENCE

Anyone who has had experience with a bipolar person knows that when the person goes into the manic phase, there are simply no controls. You can't argue logic with a manic. His energy level is beyond restraint.

But there are exceptions.

Before Bishop Wright was elevated to cardinal, he called me and said that he wanted to bring a former classmate of his to St. Francis for treatment. Father D. was a brilliant person. He had translated St. Augustine's *City of G-d* from the Latin. He was extremely well versed in classical music and was a friend of Pierre Monteux, conductor of the Los Angeles Symphony Orchestra. On occasion he would travel with the orchestra and lecture during the intermission.

Father D. had been stationed in Boston, where he enjoyed an intellectual environment. However, when he went into a manic phase, he could say things that were harmful to the church, because he was fiercely loyal to the church and could not tolerate any criticism of it. He was transferred to a much smaller community where his razor-sharp tongue could do less harm. This took him out of his intellectual environment. In this small community, there was no one on his intellectual level with whom he could communicate. He considered his new bishop as being rather dull. "In the ceremony consecrating a bishop," Father D. explained, "the priest kneels and a volume of the Bible is placed on his neck, symbolizing his acceptance of the yoke of Divine authority. This is a heavy volume, and it presses on an important nerve that goes to the brain. They are never again the same, and this is what happened to my new bishop." He bewailed this transfer, but took it in stride.

Father D.'s acceptance of Bishop Wright's authority was absolute. The bishop told him, "You must do everything Dr. Twerski instructs you." This was the first and only time a manic obeyed my orders. If he had a pass to leave the hospital for several hours and return, say, by 9:00 p.m., he would be back at 8:55. No manic can do that unless one's obedience is predominant.

Father D. used to give retreats for priests. He would tell them, "If any of you are avaricious, I will destroy you. Avarice is a sin of the soul, and there is no forgiveness for this."

Father D.'s hobby was gourmet cooking. He regretted that my kosher laws precluded my benefiting from his culinary genius.

One time, he came to Pittsburgh with a red ribbon on his collar. "They've made me a monsignor," he said, "as if that has any meaning for me. It's an effort to compensate me for removing me from Boston."

"Shall I now address you as Monsignor?" I asked.

Father D. laughed. "You wouldn't dare!" he said.

13

MY RELATIONSHIP WITH THE SISTERS

I GOT ALONG FAMOUSLY WITH THE NUNS. Someone said that this was because I reminded them of their savior, at least in their unconscious mind.

That's a possibility. When I was an intern, I treated a woman who was in a diabetic coma. She was a very devout German Catholic. When she emerged from the coma and opened her eyes, I was standing at the bedside, and she said, *"Ach, yah! Er ist schon gekommen!"* (Oh, yes! He has indeed come again!), referring to the second coming of her savior.

On one of my trips to Israel, I was at the Sea of Galilee in Tiberias. At one point, there are steps going down to the sea. I went down to the first step and had a picture taken, which gave the impression that I was walking on the water. The sisters loved it.

I used to kid the sisters, and they took it well. Sister L. was a dear, gentle soul. Sister B. was a battle-ax, and I think she was disliked by most of the sisters. One day I said to Sister L., tongue in cheek, "You know, Sister B. is going to get a much greater reward in heaven than you. You could have been someone's wife and made a man very happy. Okay, so you chose to be a nun. Sister B. will be doubly rewarded. Had she chosen to marry, she would have made some man utterly miserable. She will be handsomely rewarded for not doing this."

We rarely discussed our religious differences, but I often emphasized my belief in the inherent goodness of man, while the sisters believed in original sin. I told them that I too believe in original sin. The original sin is not to believe in the inherent goodness of man.

Sister Adele was a true saint. I told Cardinal Don Wuerl of Washington (whom I knew as Don when he was a young priest and secretary to Bishop Wright) that I will lose my respect for the church if it does not canonize her. Sister trusted me, and often consulted me on spiritual matters.

Sister Margaret was in charge of admissions. Occasionally, a patient who was under arrest required a police guard while in the hospital. However, police were not allowed to take their guns into the psychiatric unit, so they left them with Sister Margaret in the admissions office. Sister was terrified of guns and was anxious until the police left. I used to call her two-gun Peg. I don't know why they put up with me.

Sister R. was referred to me because she was depressed and cried all day. This was a simple problem to diagnose. Sister R. took care of the bishop's residence, and her crying began when the bishop was promoted to cardinal and was going to be transferred to Rome. Sister had a crush on the bishop and could not adjust to the separation.

Sister R. was not depressed. She was in *grief*. I helped her go through the five stages of grief described by Elisabeth Kubler-Ross, which can apply to any significant loss.

One nun was just a misfit. She would frequent bars and behave in ways unbecoming a nun. She had become a nun as a challenge. One time, talking with her girlfriends, she said, "I wonder what it would be like to be a nun."

"You'll never know," her friends said. "You're not even Catholic."

"I could become Catholic," she said. Sure enough, she converted and entered the convent. I helped her make a graceful exit.

One nun, who I treated for depression, felt duty bound to help everyone with their responsibilities, and she believed that relaxation was sinful indolence. She was musically talented, and I arranged for her to become a recreation counselor at a summer camp. After meals, when the staff sat around and chatted, sister would go around cleaning off all the tables. The staff said to her, "You don't have to do that. Just clean off your own table and let others clean theirs." This was a difficult adjustment for sister, but eventually she was able to stop doing other people's work. When she returned to the convent after this transformation, the sisters were very unhappy, because she no longer did their work. They said that they would no longer send their nuns to me for treatment.

Oh, well. You can't win them all.

14
VARIATIONS IN PSYCHOTHERAPY

I WAS TRAINED IN A PSYCHOANALYTIC institute in which the word of Freud was gospel. I marveled at Freud's epochal elucidation of the workings of the unconscious mind. (For some reason, the word *sub*conscious was *verboten*. We had to say *un*conscious.) We were taught that the only way one could overcome his psychological hang-ups was with formal psychoanalysis, which required four or five sessions a week for several years with a psychoanalyst. This would enable one to unearth all the memories that were hidden in the unconscious and were wreaking havoc with his emotions.

When I visited home during my first year of training, my father was interested in what I was learning. When I told him that insight-oriented, psychoanalytic psychotherapy may take several years, he was skeptical, and he told me the following story.

IN CZARIST Russia, the feudal system prevailed. Each nobleman had his fiefdom over which he had absolute rule. Most of these noblemen were ardent anti-Semites, and the Jewish population was subject to pogroms. If you've seen *Fiddler on the Roof,* you may have an idea of what a mild pogrom was like.

One nobleman, however, was a pacifist. He simply abhorred violence, and he did not allow any pogroms in his fiefdom. Some of the virulent anti-Semites in his fiefdom tried to provoke him to conduct a pogrom, but he consistently refused.

These troublemakers then fell upon an idea. This nobleman had a pet dog that was his constant companion. He loved that dog more than anything else in the world. They said to him, "Your Lordship, you know that Jews are a very shrewd people. Why, they have a way of teaching a dog how to talk, but it is a well-kept secret. They would never reveal it to you, because you are not one of them. They will never admit this. They will give you all kinds of excuses, but the truth is that they will not reveal it to you because you are a gentile."

They had found the nobleman's Achilles' heel. He called in the leaders of the Jewish community and said, "You know that I have consistently protected you. My fiefdom is the only one in which there have not been any pogroms, and you have been able to live in peace and security.

"I have one favor to ask of you, and I know that in your gratitude you will not refuse me. My dog is my constant companion. We have a way of communicating with each other, but it is limited. If my dog could talk, it would give me the opportunity to converse with him, and that would be my paradise. I know that you have a secret method of teaching a dog to talk, and I want you to grant me this one favor."

The Jewish community leaders were stymied. "Your Lordship, there is nothing in the world that we would not do for you. We owe our very lives to you, and if you would ask us to jump into a fire, we would not refuse you. However, what you are asking is the impossible. There is no such thing as teaching a dog to talk."

The nobleman became irate. "So that is how you repay me for protecting you all these years from pogroms? You are a bunch of ingrates. I will hear none of your lies and excuses. You have thirty days to teach my dog how to talk, or every single Jew, from young to old, will be driven out of my fiefdom."

"But Your Lordship—"

The nobleman interrupted, shouting, "Silence! I will hear no more! Thirty days, or expulsion. Now leave here immediately."

The Jewish community was in anguish. What could be done with this man, who was seized by a delusion that a dog can be taught to talk? Any attempt to reason with the nobleman failed. He would not allow anyone into his palace unless they had come to teach the dog to talk.

The thirtieth day was nearing, and the Jews were loading all their belongings on wagons, ready to leave the fiefdom. On the thirtieth day, one of the lesser luminaries of the community, a humble shoemaker, said, "Let me talk with the nobleman."

"Are you crazy?" the community leaders said. "He is mad with this delusion. He will not listen to our learned rabbis. What can *you* say to him?"

"What do you have to lose?" the shoemaker said. "You are ready to leave, aren't you?"

The leaders permitted him to try to reason with the nobleman, although it was certainly futile. After an hour, the shoemaker emerged from the palace with a dog on a leash. "Unpack the wagons, everybody. We're staying."

"What do you mean, 'we're staying'?" the community leaders asked. "And what are you doing with that dog?"

"I told the nobleman that I would teach his dog to talk," the shoemaker said. "I explained to His Lordship that a human child is much more intelligent than a dog. It takes about two or three years for a child to learn how to talk, so he must understand that it will take five or six years to teach a dog to talk."

"But what will happen at the end of six years?" the community leaders said.

"Relax," the shoemaker said. "During the six years, *something* is bound to happen that will extricate us from this predicament. Within six years, perhaps I will die, or the dog will die, or the nobleman will die. Within six years something will happen that will resolve this problem."

AFTER MY father finished the story, he said, "You are going to treat a patient for several years and then claim that your treatment helped him? Just think of how many things can happen in those years that may alter his life situation for the better.

"He may find a new job, he may marry, he may divorce, he may move away from meddling in-laws, his enemies may die, he may have children. Why, there is no limit to the kinds of things that may transpire during a period of several years. How can you take credit for his improvement?"

To me, this made good sense. I embraced brief psychotherapy long before the insurance companies mandated it.

I began to look into other modalities of psychotherapy, and I consider myself an eclectic therapist. I will use any technique that I think best suits the client. I did not have any formal courses in any particular therapeutic method, but sometimes, for example, when I read about a particular therapeutic technique, I realized that I had indeed been doing that.

In my approach I probably come closest to cognitive therapy. Cognitive therapy posits that a person's problems are often due to his misperception or misinterpretation of reality. I have written several books on the importance of self-awareness and self-esteem, and I believe that lack of these results in a misinterpretation of reality. Once a person misinterprets reality, one cannot make a healthy adjustment to reality.

I wrote several books on the profound psychological insights of the late Charles Schulz, creator of the *Peanuts* cartoon strip. Here is an example of Schulz's acute understanding of psychology:

1999 © Peanuts Worldwide LLC. Dist. By UNIVERSAL UCLICK.
Reprinted with permission. All rights reserved.

The little boy in the cartoon sees the world as being very dark because he assumes that he is looking through a window and not at a blackboard. Unless he can be shown that this is not a window, his perception of the world will not change. He knows what he sees—darkness—and no amount of argument will convince him that it is bright outside.

Some people, for whatever reason, misperceive the world, but they believe that what they see is reality. Cognitive therapy aims to help the person realize that one is misperceiving, and once that misperception is corrected, one can adjust properly to life. The cognitive therapist takes the little boy to a window, and shows him that the reason he saw the world as dark was because he was looking at a blackboard.

I valued my relationship with Charles Schulz, and I spent some time with him two days before he died. He had suffered a stroke during surgery for colon cancer, and this resulted in his inability to think of certain words. When he had to search for a word, he would burst into tears.

I said, "Sparky (that was his nickname), now that you've retired, you don't have to write every day. But do continue to draw cartoons, and I'll do the interpretations.

"Your ability to take complex concepts and put them into four frames of a cartoon is remarkable. Look here. In this cartoon, you have encapsulated the entire ethos of our modern culture." I then showed him the following cartoon.

1999 © Peanuts Worldwide LLC. Dist. By UNIVERSAL UCLICK. Reprinted with permission. All rights reserved.

Sally speaks for today's culture. The destination is irrelevant. What is important is that you get somewhere fast.

Modern society is obsessed with speed. The faster you do something, the better it is, even though it may be totally illogical. Automakers advertise that their car can go from zero to sixty miles per hour in 5.6 seconds. But let us think rationally. Of what practical use is that, and where can you possibly do it? But it is advertised because people do ascribe value to it.

Schulz smiled and said, "If I were to see in my cartoons what you see in them, it would paralyze me and I would not be able to draw."

A few minutes later he arose to leave. "Abe," he said, "I want you to know that I value having you as a friend." I did not realize that he was saying farewell until two days later.

THERE WAS one nun, Sister C., who was looking at a blackboard and assuming it was a window. Her convent had contacted Father Moylan because she was impossible to live with. Her perception of the world was that everything was wrong, and she always found someone to blame for what was wrong. She had been treated by a psychiatrist with medication with no result, and had been in psychotherapy for a year with no change. She negated everything the psychologist said. He was wrong too. The convent asked for a consultation with our group.

Sister C. was thirty-nine years old. Her history justified her perceiving the world as all negative. Her mother died when she was five, and she was raised in several foster homes, receiving no love whatsoever. She joined the convent in the hope of finding some love there, but she was so critical of everyone and everything that it was virtually impossible to develop positive feelings for her.

After several sessions, I realized that traditional psychotherapy would not be effective, and I decided on a novel approach. I said to Sister, "I'm going to try to help you, but not as a psychiatrist, because I don't think you are mentally ill. The reason previous treatment has not helped is because you were assumed to have some kind of mental illness. Let me tell you a story.

"You may have heard of 'the great Houdini,' a supermagician who boasted that there did not exist a lock that he could not open. They once put Houdini in a box wrapped in iron chains with multiple padlocks and threw him under the surface of an ice-covered river. A few minutes later, Houdini emerged on shore.

"One prison warden challenged Houdini, saying that he had a cell from which the magician could not escape. Houdini accepted the challenge. The warden took him to the cell and closed the door. 'I'll be in your office in five minutes or less,' Houdini said.

"Houdini used to swallow tiny instruments and regurgitate them. He began working on the lock of the cell door, expecting to open it in fifteen seconds. When he had failed to open it in forty-five seconds, he became concerned. He thought a bit, then attacked the lock anew, but was unsuccessful. Disappointed and tired, he leaned against the cell door, and it swung open. The reason he could not open the lock was because it had never been locked. The warden had played a trick on him. Even Houdini could not unlock a lock that wasn't locked in the first place.

"As doctors, we treat disease. We cannot cure a person if he's not sick. I suspect that there is no particular pathology responsible for your unhappiness. You are just discontented with the world the way it is. Disliking reality is an attitude, not a sickness. I can't treat it."

They forgot to teach me this in my psychiatric training. They taught me that all unhappiness was pathological and amenable to psychiatric treatment. If it was not treatable with medication, then we had to delve into the patient's history, especially his childhood, to find what caused him to be this way. This is indeed true in some cases, but not in all cases. People who have negative attitudes may just have to be apprised of reality.

"Here is what you must do," I said to Sister. "Every day, scan the newspapers or listen to the news for a report of some horrible happening. Then do the same for a report of some good happening, and bring these items into our sessions.

I saw Sister twice a week for thirty minutes. We went over the items she brought in, allowing her to discuss what was bad about the bad things and what was good about the good things. I did not touch on any traditional psychological material. We never discussed her childhood deprivation, only what was good and bad about the world. Very gradually, her attitude changed, and I discharged her from "treatment" after a year.

15
DELUSION AND REALITY

IN MEDICAL SCHOOL, MY PROFESSOR of pathology asked me what I intended to do after medical school, and I told him I was thinking of psychiatry. He said, "Good, good! Take all the information they give you and give it back to them on the board exams, then forget it all and use your head." He was not quite right, because I did learn many valuable things. However, I must have inherited some of my father's intuitiveness, because I did adopt some novel approaches in treatment.

My father told me about our great-uncle, the Chassidic Rebbe of Tolna, who was noted for his ability to treat psychotics. One time they brought him a paranoid psychotic who had a delusion that he was the Messiah, and nothing could budge him from this conviction.

The rebbe said to him, "Do you know who I am?"

The man answered, "Of course. You are the great Rebbe of Tolna."

"Do you not believe then that I am Divinely inspired?" the rebbe asked.

"Of course," the man said.

"Then would my Divine inspiration not reveal to me the truth, that you are the Messiah?" the Rebbe asked.

"Of course you must know that," the man agreed.

The Rebbe said, "But you see, I have taken an oath never to reveal that. You must do likewise. Never reveal that to anyone." The man promised he would never reveal it, and never again spoke of being the Messiah.

On another occasion, a lunatic threatened to jump off the roof of a tall building, and no one could talk him down. They sent for the Rebbe, who shouted up to the man, "You want to jump down from the roof? Why, any fool can do that. Come down here and show me that you can jump up to the roof." The man promptly came down.

A young man was brought to the Rebbe because he was afraid to sit down. He had a delusion that his back was made of glass, and it would break if he sat down. The rebbe told him to come back later, and in the meantime told his aide to bring a large glass bowl and a hammer. When the young man returned, the Rebbe seized him and sat him down, and this was the signal to the aide to break the glass bowl. The Rebbe showed the young man the pieces of broken glass and said, "Your glass back was broken, and now you have a normal back like everyone else." The young man was elated.

Stories like this enabled me to be innovative.

Shortly after I assumed the position at St. Francis Hospital, I was consulted by a member of the hospital board. He had a brother named Arnold who was in the army in the Korean War and had suffered a psychotic break. When he was brought back to the United States, he was admitted to a prestigious psychiatric hospital, but there was no improvement after several months. He was then transferred to the Mecca of schizophrenia treatment centers, where he had been for three years.

"I visit him every month," the board member said, "but there has been no change. Money is not the problem. We can afford to keep him there indefinitely, but if there is no treatment for him and all he can get is custodial care, he might just as well be in a Veterans Administration hospital for free." I agreed with that.

"But before we resign ourselves to custodial care, the family would like your opinion," the board member said.

"You mean that you want to bring him here from the most prestigious hospital in the country for my opinion?" I said. "I am just a neophyte in psychiatry."

"Nevertheless, we want your opinion," he said.

A few weeks later, Arnold was admitted to St. Francis Hospital, and I met him shortly after admission. He greeted me with, "Why is everyone here angry with me? I just got here. I didn't do anything to make them mad at me."

I took a deep breath and said, "Look, Arnold. You've been treated by some of the best psychiatrists in the country. If they could not cure you, I'm not even going to try.

"But I see one possibility. You said that you just got here and that you didn't do anything to cause anyone to be mad at you. That is true. That is reality. Yet, you have a feeling that they are mad you, which means that your feelings are not in keeping with the facts. You seem to be able to recognize the facts. So, if you can behave according to the facts as you see them and ignore your sick feelings, you may be able to live outside of a hospital."

Arnold seemed to take in what I said. "Oh, so that's how it is," he said.

"That's exactly how it is," I said. "Act according to the facts and ignore the feelings."

With that began a treatment I had never heard of. I came into Arnold's room, and his tray was untouched. "Aren't you hungry?" I asked.

"I can't eat. I don't have a mouth."

"That's crazy talk," I said. "You know very well that you have a mouth."

"But I don't feel—" he began saying.

I interrupted him and shouted, "I'm not interested in your feelings. They're crazy! Now you take that food and put it where you know your mouth is."

This "treatment" went on every day. Arnold would talk about his psychotic feelings, and I would shout at him that I wasn't interested in his craziness. I instructed the nurses to respond likewise. After several weeks, Arnold stopped his psychotic talk, and after three months, he was discharged. He rented an apartment near the hospital and would come to my office every day. My secretary, too, responded only to his nonpsychotic talk and ignored his psychotic talk.

I later learned that what I had done was "behavior modification." Arnold was able to live outside of a hospital.

16

GOOD HABITS

At that time, most of the sisters were still wearing their full, traditional habits. A few had begun to wear modified habits, and some had changed to civilian clothes. As an archconservative, I am opposed to changes in religion, and I let the sisters know that I was not in favor of this modernization. At a toy store, I bought a nun doll, in traditional habit, and I set it in my office with a label, "Museum of Ancient History." I warned the sisters that this was the beginning of the end for the convents. I told them that I recalled the Packard automobile, which was the car of distinction in my childhood. The Packard never changed its style. Each new model looked like the old ones, but it made a statement. Then Packard decided to go stylish and change its looks. "You don't see Packards around anymore," I said.

Father D. related that at a church picnic, there was a small child who apparently had never seen a nun before, and was frightened by their appearance. One nun picked him up, and he tried to fight her off. She spoke very softly to him, and abruptly he stopped squirming, looked at the nun, and said to his mother, "They's girls!"

The traditional habit may have been very uncomfortable, but it was a sign of distinction. Furthermore, it was a protection, because the message was, "Don't tamper with me." Once the nun was in civilian clothes, she had to be on her guard, and some of the nuns were distinctly more comfortable with the external "insect repellant."

One time, after most of the nuns had shed the traditional habit, I noticed an elderly nun in the hospital lobby in full traditional garb. I hurried to the office of Sister L., who was the administrator of the psychiatric unit, and said, "Hurry up and go into the lobby. There's a nun there!"

Sister looked at me quizzically. "So what?" she said.

"There's a nun in the lobby," I repeated. "A *real* one." I really wonder how they put up with me.

Discarding the traditional habit was not the only change. In the past, nuns were not permitted to go out alone, but had to be in pairs. Another safeguard.

One change that caused some nuns difficulty was that they were asked what they wanted to do. In the past, they would receive a little card telling them their mission for the year, that they were assigned to do the work of the L-rd at such-and-such place. They were relieved of the burden of making decisions. If they did not like their assignment, their dissatisfaction was handled by "offering it up." In other words, they were comforted by their conviction that their suffering was a sacrifice for the work of the L-rd. Secular people who are dissatisfied with their job may gripe, but they don't feel they are earning any brownie points.

One nun consulted me, handing me a questionnaire she had received about what she would like to do in the coming year. She felt totally bewildered. "I don't know what I want to do next year; I just want to know where I'm needed."

Some nuns could not adjust to the changes and left the convent. I learned that they were referred to as "fugitives." I was upset by this, and I told the bishop that it was unfair for a woman who gave the twenty best years of her life to the church to be referred to as a fugitive. The bishop sent word that this term was not to be used. This endeared me to the sisters.

I found that the nuns could essentially be divided into groups. There were the elderly nuns, who were set in their ways and paid little attention to the liberalizing changes in religious life. There were the young women, who entered in the era of the changes, and were essentially satisfied.

Then there was the group between forty and sixty years of age, who had entered the convent under one set of rules, and now found that this was not quite what they had asked for. Some were uncomfortable with the changes. They were accustomed to the old rules, to which they had made a commitment. Should they remain under the new conditions? On the other hand, what would they do if they left? Marriage was not a great option. They were older, and past childbearing age. Some were resentful, because if they had the option when they were in their twenties, they might have chosen a family life.

These sisters needed an objective listening ear, which we provided. We were certainly not judgmental, and we sympathized with their predicament. Most elected to stay, but a few left. We continued to provide support for both.

It was inevitable that during these sessions, issues arose that had nothing to do with religious life, issues that were no different from those of lay people. We dealt with these as well. All in all, the service we provided was deeply appreciated, and the nuns felt that the church was indeed looking out for their best interests.

17

TWO FASCINATING CASES

Early in my psychiatric training, I had a patient who suffered from disabling anxiety. All of the treatment she had received with many hours of psychotherapy had not helped. In addition, we did not have the medications we have today. I was upset in being unable to help her, and my ego could not take a failure. I asked her, "Would you consider hypnosis?"

"I would consider anything to be free of this anxiety," she answered.

I told her to rethink this for several days, because I did not have the faintest idea how to induce a hypnotic trance. I was once hypnotized during my internship, so I felt there was nothing wrong with hypnosis.

I went to the library and read a book on medical hypnosis. Fortunately, one of my buddies was competent in hypnosis and I consulted him. I was just careful not to make any foolish suggestions. I essentially allowed the patient to express her emotions under hypnosis. After only a few sessions, she had remarkable relief of her anxiety.

Throughout her therapy, this patient had responded to all my interpretations and insights with, "I understand everything, but it just doesn't help me feel better." I think that what happened was that all the insights she gained were intellectual, but there was a barrier to emotional insight. The hypnotic experience broke through the barrier. It was similar to water backing up behind a dam. One small hole in the dam allowed all the backed-up water to flow through.

I began to use hypnosis more frequently and became quite adept at it. In competent hands and in well-chosen cases, it can be a valuable adjunct to therapy. It can help in relief of chronic pain. However, it should not be expected to be a magic wand.

I will relate two rather dramatic cases in which hypnosis was helpful.

The first case was a thirty-four-year-old nun, who called me saying, "I have a severe dermatitis, and have had treatment for years, but nothing is working. I was told that it could be emotional, and I saw a psychiatrist several times, but the convent could not afford his fees. I was recently transferred here, and I wonder whether I could be treated at St. Francis."

I told Sister that I would be glad to see her, but that I needed a consultation from a local dermatologist to know what I was dealing with. I referred her to a local dermatologist who had an interest in psychology. After seeing her, he called me. "She has a total body eczema," he said. "She is on high doses of cortisone, and there is nothing more I can do for her."

I asked the patient whether anything caused it to be worse or if anything relieved it. She said, "If I have a strict superior, it gets worse. The last superior that I had, she really *got under my skin.*" (Freud would have had a field day with that.) She then said that when she bathed in the ocean, she felt better, but she did not live near the ocean.

My associate, Dr. Naar, and I decided to give hypnosis a try. Unfortunately, Sister was weak with visual imagery. She could not picture a scene in her mind. So we had her imagine she was on the beach, feeling the sand and the warmth of the sun, tasting the salt on her lips, and smelling the iodine in the air. We then had her go into the water and swim for ten minutes while still in a hypnotic trance.

Sister returned three days later, saying that she thought she felt a bit better. Dr. Naar repeated the hypnotic session, and on the next visit she said that she definitely felt better. He then taught her self-hypnosis, and that three times a day she was to put herself into a trance and "swim in the ocean" for ten to fifteen minutes. A week later, there was unquestionable improvement. I then had her reduce the cortisone from four to three times daily. She continued to swim in the trance, and by the end of four weeks, her skin was totally clear and she was completely off the cortisone.

I sent her back to the dermatologist, who called me, saying that if he had read the account of this case in a medical magazine, he would not have believed it. He invited Sister to his Passover seder (ritual meal) and gave her a necklace with a Star of David.

"Why did you do that?" I asked.

"So we'll have a Jewish nun," he replied.

I cannot explain why she was cured. One can construct many theories. One thing is certain: it was not due to the chemicals in the ocean water. I have no doubt that her statement "she really got under my skin" indicated that scratching was an expression of anger at whatever or whoever had gotten "under her skin," but we never dealt directly with her feelings of anger.

The second case was a bit more complicated. This was a nun who had been treated by several psychiatrists for severe depression, with no results. One psychologist felt that she had repressed anger and told her to discharge her anger by breaking empty bottles. There is a mistaken belief that the way to get rid of pent-up anger is to discharge it by screaming, breaking things, or hitting a punching bag. This actually *increases* the anger.

On one visit, she was accompanied by her superior, who asked her, "Did you tell the doctor about Elaine?" whereupon Sister burst into tears.

Sister then related that when she was twelve, her mother had left her to care for her younger sister, Elaine, who was four. They were playing tag. And she was running after the child, who was holding a collapsed rubber balloon between her teeth. The child aspirated the balloon and was asphyxiated, dying in her arms. She had not been able to forgive herself for this. She sought religious absolution, but to no avail. After multiple confessions, the priest told Sister to consult a psychiatrist. "I feel guilty for her death," she said.

"Why would you feel guilty?" I asked. "You were in no way responsible for what happened."

"I know," she said, "but I still feel it was my fault."

I then decided on a radical tactic. I would hypnotize her and regress her to the day of this incident, then try to extirpate the incident as though it never happened. I was going to change her reality. I had read where Professor Milton Erickson, the dean of hypnotherapy, had done something similar.

I called Professor Erickson in Phoenix, Arizona, and told him of my plan.

"Dr. Twerski, that is absolutely insane!" he said.

"But you did something similar," I said.

Erickson said, "That is absolutely insane, but let me know what happens."

I hypnotized Sister and successfully regressed her to the day of the incident. Here is what she related in the hypnotic trance.

"I'm sweeping the floor. My mother said that I couldn't have my friends over unless I cleaned up the house. I'm sweeping the stairs to the cellar. Elaine is standing at the head of the stairs, saying, 'Come play with me.' I said I couldn't because I have to clean up the house. Elaine picks up the throw rug and throws it at me. I'm so angry at her. I run up after her. She giggles and runs outside, and I run after her."

(Note: When she related the incident to me, she said that they were playing tag. Reliving the incident revealed that they were not playing tag at all, but that she was running after Elaine to hit her.)

Sister continued, "Elaine runs into the alley, and I shout, 'Stop, Elainy, stop!'"

I interrupted her. "Why are you shouting at her to stop?"

"Because she might get hit by a car in the alley," she said.

I said, "Look. You were running after her to punish her, but you stopped her from running into the alley because you were afraid she might be hit by a car. You didn't want her to die. Do you see? You wanted to punish her, but you didn't want her to die."

I repeated this several times, stressing that although she was angry at her, she did stop her from running into the alley because she did not want her to die.

Sister then continued to describe the incident of the asphyxiation, crying bitterly. After the narration, I brought her back to the present and ended the trance. The first thing she said was, "Yes, I wanted to hit her, but I did not want her to die." Sister gradually recovered from her depression.

What had happened with Sister was that the child died while she was trying to punish her. Her mind associated the two, so that she felt that in her anger, she had killed her. It was fortunate that she had stopped her from running into the alley, so that she could see that although she was angry at her, she tried to protect her from harm. Once the death was detached from the anger, her guilt was relieved.

Sister recovered completely from her depression. Becoming a nun may have been an effort to expiate the unjustified guilt. I did not have any follow-up whether Sister remained in the convent.

18

MORE REAL THAN REALITY

AFTER THE STORY OF THE REMARKABLE recovery of the nun from a chronic dermatitis via hypnosis made its way around the hospital, one of the secretaries asked if I could treat her for a similar problem. Carol was a fantastic hypnotic subject, and had complete relief from her dermatitis. The hospital staff then asked if I would do a demonstration of the medical uses of hypnosis. I asked Carol if she would volunteer to serve as the subject in the demonstration, and she readily agreed.

I hypnotized Carol in front of the medical staff, and I demonstrated age regression, anesthesia, and taste sensation. I asked Carol if she would like to eat an orange, and she said, "Sure." I then showed her a lemon and told her it was an orange. I cut it and gave it to her. She ate the lemon, saying it was delicious, and the staff was grimacing.

I showed the staff that one can induce hallucinations with hypnosis. I had her close her eyes, and I put a chair at her right. I told her that when she opened her eyes, she would see Betty, one of her friends in the secretarial pool, sitting at her right. She opened her eyes, turned to the empty chair, and began a conversation with the hallucinated Betty.

"What are you doing here?" Carol asked. "Didn't you go home after work?" After receiving an auditory hallucinated answer, Carol said, "Oh, you wanted to stay for the show," and she continued their dialogue.

Looking up at the audience, I saw that the real Betty had indeed stayed for the show. I had Carol close her eyes, and I put another chair on her left. I signaled to Betty to sit at Carol's left, then I told Carol to open her eyes and continue talking to Betty. She turned to her right and continued her conversation with the hallucinated Betty.

I then went to her left and said, "Carol, look here."

Carol turned to her left and reacted with shock. She looked back and forth to her right and left. "How can Betty be in two places?" she asked.

"Carol, I'm playing a trick on you," I said. "There is only one real Betty. The other is make-believe. I want you to look at both Bettys and tell me which is the real one."

Carol looked back and forth several times, then pointed to the empty chair at her right. "This is the real Betty," she said.

I told the staff that they had just witnessed a powerful psychological phenomenon. "A hallucination is more real than reality." This is why it is fruitless to try to convince a psychotic that his visions and voices are not real. To him, they are more real than reality.

19
A NON-NARCOTIC PAINKILLER

Carol wasn't the only one in the hospital who approached me as a result of the successful treatment of the nun through hypnosis. One doctor who was treating Sister T. for metastatic cancer contacted me. The sister was receiving chemotherapy. Her appetite was poor and she was losing weight. Worst of all, she had severe pain, and refused heavy doses of narcotics because it clouded her mind. She was a bright woman and could not tolerate feeling befuddled. "Do you think you could give her some pain relief with hypnosis?" the doctor asked me.

"I don't know, but I can try," I said.

Hypnosis can indeed provide pain relief. Major surgical procedures have been performed with the patient under hypnosis without any anesthetic at all. However, the patient must be able to achieve a deep level of hypnosis, and hypnotizability varies from person to person.

Sister T. was brought to the office in a wheelchair. She did her best to smile, but was obviously depressed, as could be expected for someone in her condition.

I tried to induce a hypnotic trance, but in two attempts, Sister could enter only a shallow level of hypnosis. In an effort to deepen the trance, I told Sister to try to picture any enjoyable experience she had. After a few moments, I saw her smile. "Can you tell me what you are experiencing?" I asked.

"I'm riding horseback," she said. "Please don't talk to me now."

After about ten minutes, Sister opened her eyes. "That was fun," she said. "As a young girl, my father took me horseback riding. His uncle had a farm with several horses. I enjoyed the horses. I felt I could communicate with them. As often as he could, my father took me to Uncle Oswald's farm, and I rode the horses."

I repeated this at the next session, but to my disappointment, reliving these pleasant moments did not deepen the hypnotic trance anywhere near the level necessary to achieve pain relief. However, since the experience was so enjoyable, I taught Sister how to put herself into a hypnotic trance and relive the horseback riding and any other pleasant experiences she could think of.

Amazingly, Sister's appetite improved and she regained some weight. She was even able to get around without a wheelchair. She said that her pain was much less severe and could be relieved with small doses of medication that did not affect the clarity of her mind.

Unfortunately, Sister T.'s cancer progressed, and after about a year she died. However, the quality of her life had been greatly enhanced by her hypnotic recall of horseback riding.

I'm sure that we all had enjoyable experiences in our youth. Sometimes, we encounter hardships in life that are depressing. If we can learn to relive those enjoyable experiences, with or without hypnosis, we may be able to elevate our spirits and cope more effectively with the problems we encounter in life.

20

MIND-BODY RELATIONSHIP

When I was in medical school, psychiatry and psychology were given token recognition. Everything was physical. The causes of disease were all physical—infection, trauma, tumor; diagnosis was physical—laboratory, X-ray, electrocardiogram; and treatment was physical—medication, surgery. There was no denying that human beings had a mind, but the functioning of the mind was not the legitimate concern of physicians. Oh, there were a few "shrinks" who were tolerated, but the role of the mind in health was ignored.

When I told my professor of pharmacology that I intended to become a psychiatrist, he said, "A waste of a medical education. Before long we will develop a pill that will put you all out of business."

How ironic. The greater part of my practice was treating people who had become addicted to the pharmacological "miracle" drugs: painkillers, tranquilizers, stimulants, and sleeping pills. Psychiatry was promoting the concept of psychosomatic medicine, that genuine physical illnesses could be the result of emotions, but for the greater part, the medical establishment dismissed this. Today, every doctor knows that emotions and stress can cause or contribute to high blood-pressure, heart disease, and digestive disorders. There is convincing evidence for the role of emotions in the genesis of cancer.

There are many studies that show that an upbeat emotional state can positively affect the recovery from cancer and that depression can hinder recovery from many diseases. Let me share one case with you.

In 1970 I received a call from a man in Cleveland asking for an appointment. I told him that I don't treat people from out of town and that there are many fine psychiatrists in Cleveland. He pleaded, "No, it has to be you. I'll come even at two o'clock in the morning." I agreed to see him.

This was a thirty-nine-year-old man who consulted his doctor for a minor infection. Upon getting the results of a routine blood test, the doctor told him, "You are going directly from here to the oncologist's office." A bone marrow test revealed that he had a form of leukemia and was given an eighteen-month prognosis. "I cry all day," the man said.

I felt very deeply for the man, and I said to him, "As a psychiatrist, I can treat depression when the depression is an illness, but your depression is not an illness. It is a normal reaction to such a devastating illness. Anti-depression medication does not relieve this kind of depression. I wish I knew how to help you."

"And another thing," the man said, "is that I have to go to the hospital every two weeks for tests, and I am deathly afraid of hospitals."

"Although I can't do much for your depression, I can help you with your phobia of hospitals." I planned to use what is known as systematic desensitization, which is particularly effective with the help of hypnosis.

I began treating his phobia with hypnosis. When he was in a hypnotic trance, an idea occurred to me. I told him to visualize a happy occasion that he had experienced, perhaps a wedding or a bar mitzvah. He was able to visualize the scene, to hear the music, and see the dancing. I dwelt on this and told him, "You are going to deposit these feelings of joy in your mind. Each time you visualize a happy scene, you will add to the feelings of happiness that will be stored in your mind. You will deposit these feelings in your mind just as you deposit money into your bank account.

"Just as you can withdraw money from your bank account, you can withdraw feelings of happiness from the account in your mind. Your withdrawal slip is the word *simchah* (happiness). When you say the word *simchah*, that will be a signal to your mind to produce the feeling of happiness." In order to be able to make repeated withdrawals, you must replenish the account with repeated deposits." I taught him self-hypnosis, and three times a day he was to put himself in a trance for ten to fifteen minutes and experience a joyous scene.

Eighteen months passed, then two years, then three years. His oncologist said, "Jay, I don't know what on earth you're doing, but do more of it."

It is now forty-two years since this man was given a prognosis of eighteen months to live. I am still in occasional contact with him. There is now proof that the immune system is subject to emotional influence. I believe that the upbeat spirit that he was able to generate and maintain influenced his immune system to suppress the leukemia.

21

NOT MENTALLY ILL

Being the director of psychiatry at St. Francis Hospital provided me with an invaluable education. For all intents and purposes, St. Francis served as the psychiatric emergency service for the tristate area—Pennsylvania, Ohio, and West Virginia. Understandably, the emergency room was very, very busy.

People have the idea that all unusual behavior is due to mental illness. However, there are many physical problems that can produce mental symptoms, and if the correct diagnosis is overlooked, the results may be disastrous. After several years at St. Francis, I wrote a book entitled *Who Says You're Neurotic?* reporting a variety of cases where the strange behavior was due to physical conditions, among them meningitis, kidney failure, hypoglycemia (low blood sugar), stroke, and brain tumors.

An eighty-two-year-old nun was brought for psychiatric admission one evening because she was hallucinating. She was seeing cats all over the place, on the walls and on the ceiling. There was no history of mental illness. She had been perfectly normal until that day.

It should have been evident that a person who was perfectly normal for eighty-two years and has a sudden onset of bizarre behavior is not mentally ill. Mental illness develops more slowly.

Earlier that day, this Sister had her eyes examined by an ophthalmologist, who put drops in her eyes to dilate her pupils. Perhaps due to her advanced age, she was so sensitive to chemicals that the eyedrops were toxic to her brain, and she had toxic hallucinations. She was given a sedative and a nun sat with her to reassure her that she was okay. When she woke up the next morning, she was no longer hallucinating.

A mistaken diagnosis of mental illness may be a serious mistake, not only because the physical problem is overlooked, but if this mistake is made on a younger person, and the chart has a diagnosis of a mental illness, this person may be wrongfully labeled as mentally ill, and that label may haunt him/her for the rest of his/her life. This is virtually impossible to undo, because once a person is thought to be mentally ill, people cannot be reassured that he/she is perfectly normal.

22

I'M NOT ANGRY

IN THE SIXTEENTH CENTURY, THERE WAS a physician in Basel, Switzerland, by the name of Paracelsus, who gathered all his students in front of a bonfire and said, "Throw all your medical books into the fire. If you want to learn medicine, go study your patients."

Today's medical books do have value, yet Paracelsus's statement does have some truth. We learn much from our patients.

When I entered psychiatric training, not much was known about the biological causes of mental illness. All psychiatric illness was thought to be due to life experiences; i.e., to psychological causes. We were taught that depression was due to "internalized rage." In the next few years, medications were found that treated depression, and electroshock treatment relieved severe depressions. Probably most severe depressions are of biochemical origin. However, there may be depressions that are indeed due to internalized rage.

Sister A.M. suffered from chronic depression. Medications and electroshock were of no avail. I tried to work with her in psychotherapy, but I wasn't getting anywhere either.

One day, I received a call from Milwaukee that my mother was hospitalized, and I left immediately. I called the patients who had appointments and canceled them. When I returned, my secretary told me that Sister A.M. had come for her appointment. I had neglected to notify her of the cancellation. I called to reschedule her appointment. I really felt bad, because Sister A.M. did not drive, and she had to take two buses to get to the hospital. The bus schedule was such that she had to travel an hour and a half for her appointment. On the day I was gone, she waited in the lobby for an hour beyond her appointment time, and only then did she discover that I was not there that day.

When I next saw her, I apologized for my negligence, but Sister said, "That's okay."

"It's not okay," I said. "You wasted half a day because I did not have the courtesy to call you to cancel the appointment. I'm sure that when you found out that I wasn't here, you were furious."

"Why should I be angry?" Sister said. "I know that doctors get called out on emergencies. I wasn't angry."

I said, "Sister, don't make excuses for me. I'll make my own. Don't tell me you weren't angry when you found that you had wasted half a day."

"No," Sister said, "I wasn't angry."

I then realized what had happened. In her training, Sister was taught that anger is a terrible sin, and she learned to repress it. I now understood why all treatment for her depression had failed. She did not have a biochemical depression. Her depression was the "internalized anger," and this had to be dealt with.

As a young girl, Sister had been extremely insecure. She had an inferiority complex, considering herself unlikable and undesirable company. Even with her parents she constantly did things to earn their approval, of which there was never enough for her. She developed a pattern of trying to please people, hoping that by accommodating to everyone's wishes she would acquire their friendship and love.

Sister had never dated. Having chosen religious life in early adolescence, she felt herself incapable of being loved by a man, and by eschewing male companionship, she avoided what she felt would be inevitable and painful rejection.

In addition to believing that she was unworthy of being loved, Sister's feelings of inadequacy also resulted in her distrust of her ability to control her feelings. For her to feel anger was frightening as well as sinful. If she could not control her anger, expressing it would alienate people.

Religious life provided a solution to two important conflicts. First, Sister felt that she would be able to have the security and stability that other women might normally expect in marriage, and by being a nun she would avoid the loneliness and perhaps the stigma of being a spinster. Secondly, she envisioned convent life as one where there is unconditional acceptance, where she could avoid the fear of rejection, and where repression of anger is reinforced and considered a virtue.

I proceeded to tell Sister that she had misunderstood what she had been taught. The correct teaching was that *reacting* in anger was a sin, but not the *feeling* of anger. One has no choice whether or not to feel anger when provoked, and something over which one has no control cannot be a sin. It took several sessions to undo her misconception, and to realize that it is only natural to *feel* anger, but one must be careful how one acts when angry. Sister's depression gradually lifted.

One day Sister told me that she was very angry because the priest at her parish was being transferred to another church. "I'm not going to play the organ anymore," she said.

"Sister, you have every right to feel angry," I said, "but by refusing to play the organ, you are acting out your anger, and that is what you were taught is wrong."

I learned something very valuable from Sister. If depression does not respond to medication, one should consider the possibility that it may be internalized anger.

I also learned something else. Sister's inability to feel anger when I had not notified her of my absence was because this affected her personally. The anger at the transfer of the priest was something she could accept, because it was righteous indignation at a deprivation of the entire parish. Therefore, it was justifiable. It also indicated how foolish we may act when enraged. Who was going to suffer from her refusal to play the organ? Not whoever in the diocese made the decision to transfer the priest, but the very parish she was seeking to defend.

In my twenty years at St. Francis Hospital, I attended a variety of meetings with the administrator, Sister Adele. There were times when she was provoked in a way that would have made someone else furious, but she kept her poise. A day or so later, Sister would say to me, "You know, that person at the meeting really made me angry."

"I know, Sister," I would say.

"You mean I showed it?" she said.

"No. You did an excellent job of concealing it."

"Then how did you know?" she asked.

"Why do you think I am a psychiatrist?"

Another aspect of anger was demonstrated by Brother X., a Benedictine monk. Brother X. had a most pleasant personality. He was very sensitive, always smiling. I can't even recall why he came to see me. All I can recall is nonclinical conversations. He used to tell me how he gathers mushrooms in the woods and offered to teach me how to distinguish good mushrooms from poisonous ones.

Brother X. did not have repressed anger. He was well aware of his anger at the nuns who were his teachers in grade school. "I was ten years old and she kept telling me that I am guilty of having sinful thoughts. What kind of sinful thoughts could

I have had at age ten? There were several other nun teachers who were simply mean. I made a decision to become a priest in order to show the world that the church is not cruel."

At the close of each session, Brother X. would bow his head and say, "Bless me, rabbi."

23
KNOW YOUR SKILLS

ONE NUN WHO HAD MADE GREAT progress in overcoming her depression came in to my office one time quite anxious. She was a mathematics teacher for a middle school and had received an assignment for the oncoming semester to teach a class of slow learners. Sister felt very uncomfortable about this. She did not have any training in teaching slow learners, but if she refused this assignment, it would be a violation of her vow of obedience.

Teaching a child who has limitations can be gratifying if one is satisfied with getting the child to perform at his/her maximum. However, not everyone can be satisfied with this. There are some people who must see tangible results. They are happy when they have enabled a student to use algebra in solving problems, but slightly increasing a child's ability to read is not a sufficient accomplishment to please them, although they may have enabled the child to reach his maximum potential.

I knew Sister's personality. She was not a person who could be happy with small increases in a child's progress. Teaching a class of slow learners would be frustrating for her and she would not succeed with these students.

I offered to call Sister's superiors and explain why this particular assignment was not in her best interests or that of the students. Sister was greatly relieved, and she received a more appropriate assignment. At the end of the semester I received a thank-you card that read, "Thank you for relieving my depression and preserving my sanity."

24

A SERIOUS REGRET

SISTER R. WAS A FORTY-YEAR-OLD NUN who was referred to us for depression. Father Moylan, who referred her to our service, said, "Sister is not depressed. She is just unhappy."

There are many depressions that are primarily due to neurohormonal changes in the body rather than to psychological causes. Any stress to the body, e.g., severe virus, surgery, or the hormonal changes incident to childbirth or menopause, can cause a biochemical depression. Biochemical depressions may also be of genetic origin. These are best treated with medications that can correct the chemical imbalance. Groping in the patient's history for psychological causes may sometimes be counterproductive.

Father Moylan's observation that Sister was unhappy rather than depressed was right on target. She had not responded to antidepressant medication because there was no chemical imbalance for the medication to correct.

Sister said that she became a nun to please her family, who were devout Catholics. One brother was a priest, as was an uncle. Sister said that she gave up marriage and a family life as a sacrifice which she "offered up" to G-d. She was uncomfortable with the liberal changes in the convent and was contemplating leaving. "They had no right to change the rules after I had made a commitment," she said. Projecting her dissatisfaction on the changes in religious life was clearly a defensive maneuver.

"I am forty, pretty much beyond childbearing age. I am not a prime choice for marriage. Who would want to marry an ex-nun? So what am I sacrificing for? I could have been married and had a family." Her disappointment was understandable.

However, Sister's attributing her choice of a religious life to please the family or get their approval was not completely correct. She said that in her adolescence and early adulthood she was not interested in dating, thinking men to be self-centered and inconsiderate. A bit of further investigation revealed that this was not quite true. She did have a desire for a relationship with a male, but was afraid that she would be disappointed. Joining the convent removed this worry.

Sister was very self-conscious and felt uneasy in social settings, fearing rejection. The convent provided a safe haven for her. The truth was that her choice of a religious life was hardly the sacrifice she made it out to be, and even now, the convent was a more comfortable place than the secular world.

Sister's uneasiness in social settings and her fear of rejection were due to very low self-esteem. Having these negative feelings about herself, she assumed that other people would consider her undesirable and would not want to associate with her. Being a nun would give her some distinction and relieve some of her low self-esteem.

Sister was referred to a therapy group and did very well. While she was initially very angry with herself for having made the wrong choice in life, the insights she gathered about herself reduced the anger appreciably. The changes in convent life were excuses, and she eventually made peace with remaining a nun.

25

THE FUGITIVE

In previous days, Sister O. would have been called a fugitive. That term was eliminated by order of the bishop. But although the convent no longer referred to nuns who left the community as fugitives, Sister O. did think of herself in those terms.

Sister O. was a young woman who was a disciple of Sister N., an older nun who took her under her wing from the moment she entered the convent, and they had a mother-daughter relationship. It was rare to see one not in the presence of the other.

One day, Sister N. said to me, "I'm very concerned about Sister O. I don't know whether she is depressed or what. She is withdrawing from me."

I was on good terms with Sister O., so I arranged to see her. Sister O. was relieved to unburden herself. She told me the following: "I haven't said anything to Sister N., because it would kill her. I'm really not certain of this myself, but I've taken an interest in a man. We meet stealthily, and I think I love him, and I am considering leaving the community. But since there is nothing definite, I didn't want to tell Sister N. Why have her worry unnecessarily? It might turn out to be nothing."

I told Sister O. that she was not covering it up very well. "Sister N. is already worried. I suggest you be open with her. If you decide to leave the community, it will not come as a shock. If you stay, she can be very supportive of you."

"But I know that Sister N. will discourage me and do a guilt trip with me. I don't need that," Sister O. said.

"Nevertheless, I don't think you should keep secrets from her," I said.

About two months later, Sister O. told me that she had decided to leave the community. She told Sister N. about it, and Sister N.'s reaction was as I suspected. She cried bitterly and went into a depressed state, like any mother who has lost a daughter. This was grief rather than a depression, and Sister N. came out of it in time.

Sister O., who was now Jeanette, married the man. She did call me to tell me that she was happily married.

I received a call from a former nun from a different order. "I'm no longer with the convent. Can I still come to see you?" she asked. "I can't afford a psychiatrist." I did not consult the diocese and decided to see her.

Nora had left the convent and had married, but before too long, the honeymoon was over. "When I was a nun, Frank looked up to me and respected me," she said, "but now it's just the opposite. I can't do anything right. He puts me down and calls me insulting names. I left the convent, to which I had made a sacred vow, just for him. That was a sacrifice, but he has no appreciation for it.

"I should not have left the convent for Frank. I know that you influenced the bishop to eliminate the term 'fugitive,' but that's what I think I am.

"I don't know what to do. I'm still Catholic, and I don't believe in divorce, but I can't tolerate being put down all the time. I made a wrong decision by leaving the community, and I don't want to make another wrong decision now.

"I not only messed up my life, but I know what my leaving the community did to some of the other sisters. I can't live with my guilt."

I asked Nora whether Frank would come to see me. She said she did not know, but would ask him.

Frank did not want the marriage to fail, and agreed to therapy. I was able to arrange therapy for both of them. Nora had some issues to deal with, including that she had disappointed her superior.

I was updated a year later, and the marriage was intact and satisfactory to both.

26
GUILT

It is said that the Jews invented guilt and the Catholics perfected it. It makes much sense for a problem of guilt to be addressed by both a rabbi and a priest.

Needless to say, having taken vows of chastity, obedience, and poverty, many of the sisters expressed guilt in their failure to live up to their vows, at least emotionally.

I told the sisters that there are two types of guilt, healthy and unhealthy. Healthy guilt is when a person has violated a moral or ethical principle. The guilt over such actions is a deterrent to their performance, and also motivates a person to take appropriate corrective steps to atone or make amends for the misdeed. If a person does not feel guilt for doing something wrong, that is a serious failure of conscience.

However, there may be unwarranted feelings of guilt, in which case the guilt is pathologic. For example, in the case of the story of the nun who could not rid herself of the guilt for her sister's death, that guilt was pathologic. There was no reason why she deserved to feel guilty over the child's accidental death, and the guilt was the result of a psychological quirk, which disappeared when the latter was resolved.

The religious procedures to attain forgiveness are effective only for healthy guilt. Pathologic guilt requires therapy. The priest who heard the nun's confession about her guilt over her younger sister's death wisely told her to consult a psychologist.

I told the sisters that a person may legitimately feel guilty only for doing something over which one had control. There should be no guilt feelings for things a person cannot control.

One does not have the control to prevent emotional feelings, but he is duty bound to avoid harboring or expressing improper emotions.

Thus, if one experiences an aggressive urge, he should not feel guilty about this, because one does not have the control to avoid it. However, one should do the utmost to distract oneself from a forbidden urge. If one does not do so, but willfully harbors the improper emotion, then there is legitimate reason for guilt. As was noted in the case of the nun who did not allow herself to feel anger, repressing unwanted feelings can result in emotional disorders.

Religious teachings can help minimize a person's sensitivity to provocations, but they cannot completely eliminate it. We can develop techniques to distract ourselves from undesirable thoughts and feelings, and if we do not use these, but allow ourselves to harbor improper thoughts and feelings and fantasize about them, there may be healthy guilt, for which absolution should be sought.

I told the sisters that the occurrence of feelings that are prohibited by their vows is likely to continue throughout life. G-d created many angels, who are wholly spiritual beings and have no animalistic drives. He did not intend for human beings to be angels, totally devoid of physical urges. Rather, He wanted human beings to be masters of their urges, and this is a duty that continues throughout one's life.

Father Moylan concurred in this approach to guilt. The rabbi and the priest worked together to address a frequent problem among nuns.

27

KLEPTOMANIA

Sister V. sat down in my office and broke into tears. "I'm so terribly ashamed," she said. "I can't stand it. I wish I were dead."

I sat silently by, until Sister calmed down. "I'm a thief," she said. "A nun and a thief."

After a brief silence, Sister said, "It started when I was about eleven. I'd pick up things in a store. Stupid things, like a ring I never wore or a pencil I didn't need. Sometimes I would go back to the store and put it back. Sometimes I'd just throw it away. It's just so crazy, but I couldn't help myself. It wasn't something I did regularly. Months could go by when I wouldn't steal anything, but I knew that another theft was just around the corner.

"When I joined the convent and put on the nun's habit, that kept me from stealing. I was afraid of the shame it would bring to the convent if I were caught. Now that we can wear civilian clothes, that deterrent isn't there, and I've started doing it again. I don't know why I do it."

I explained to Sister that kleptomania is an impulse control disorder whose cause remains a mystery. Because kleptomania is often associated with other psychiatric disorders, I asked

Sister about other symptoms she might have, but I did not detect any. Her childhood history was quite bland.

"Have you ever shared this with anyone?" I asked. Sister said that she had confessed it several times.

I did not feel that traditional psychotherapy would be of much help. Medications are of little value in kleptomania. Although some think it to be a variety of OCD, it does not respond to medications the way OCD does.

I said to Sister, "What I am going to tell you may seem difficult or even impossible for you. I want you to join a therapy group. You see, there is a principle that we are as sick as the secrets we keep.

"Keeping a secret is a source of stress, because we live in fear of being found out. The stress becomes a contributing factor to persistence of the problem. Once we are relieved of this stress. it is easier to bring the symptom under control.

"I don't expect you to blurt out your problem in your first session, but I want you to attend the group. You can remain silent or you can talk about other issues you have. Perhaps sometime in the future you may feel comfortable sharing your problem with the group."

Sister did join the group and felt much at ease. For about eight sessions, she did not bring up the kleptomania. During this time, she heard other members of the group share a variety of problems, and this gave her the courage to talk about her kleptomania. She was pleasantly surprised at the group's reaction, which was supportive and understanding. Some offered to accompany Sister when she does her shopping.

Months later, Sister stopped at my office. "I've never before felt so free. I haven't had the desire to pick up anything for a long time," she told me.

28
OBEDIENCE VERSUS CONTROL

I received a call from Father Moylan. "I'm sorry to put this one on you, Dr. Twerski," he said, "because it's a religious issue that I should be able to handle. There's a rather young nun who is giving the convent a hard time with obedience. She understands the nature of the vow but still insists on doing things the way she wants to."

Sister O. was a twenty-eight-year-old woman. She said she was glad to have the opportunity to discuss the problem with me. "I know I'm giving the convent a hard time. I don't want to be rebellious, but I end up being defiant. I understand that I surrendered my will to the L-rd. That is a vow I made with full knowledge of what it meant, and I don't for a minute regret having made it. I believe that the will of the L-rd is made known to us through our superiors, and I know I should accept it, but I can't seem to control my defiant attitude."

I took a basic history of Sister O. Her mother died when she was four, and a few years later her father remarried. "My stepmother is really a nice person and I do like her, but she was very controlling. Everything had to be her way. She dominated my father as well as us kids. I got to resent her controlling me. It became pretty intolerable. Whether she was dominating to me or to my father or to my siblings, it made no difference. The tone of her voice would send me into orbit.

"I knew that by entering religious life I would have to surrender my will to that of the L-rd, but that was my own choice, so it's actually an extension of my own will to do His will. I want to be obedient. Still, when I'm told that I have to do something, I get a knee-jerk reaction of defiance. Even if I do as I'm told, I bristle with resentment, but sometimes I don't listen, and even if I do, I often mouth off."

I explained to Sister that the greater part of our minds is the subconscious, and the subconscious is like the hard drive of a computer, on which every experience we have ever had is recorded, and nothing is automatically deleted. Many thoughts and feelings are relegated to the subconscious, where they are stored indefinitely. We are generally unaware of what is stored in the subconscious.

"All the instances in which your stepmother controlled you are recorded on the hard drive of your subconscious, along with the emotions that accompanied them. You may have built up a huge deposit of resentment to being controlled by her. Anytime you now feel you are in any way being controlled, that activates all the memories that are stored in your subconscious of your stepmother's control and the resentment associated with them. So if someone orders you to do something, that triggers the pent-up feelings in the subconscious, and you react, not to the order you've just been given, but rather to the avalanche of feelings that have accumulated in the subconscious.

"If you could dissociate the two, you could more easily be obedient according to your vows. When you are defiant, you are not responding to what you were ordered to do now, but to the pent-up feelings that accumulated over the years."

However, I must point out that obedience is a major challenge, and it may be a lifetime struggle. The Talmud cites a dialogue between the Roman satrap Antonine and the sage Rabbi Judah as to when the evil inclination enters a person. Rabbi Judah said that this occurs at the moment of conception. Antonine disagreed. "If a fetus had an evil inclination it would kick its way out of its mother's womb." Rabbi Judah conceded the point.

But why would the fetus kick its way out of the womb? It has no desire for physical pleasures, and if it left the womb, it would die. The answer is that the prime thrust of the evil inclination is not, as we may think, indulging in physical pleasures. *The evil inclination refuses to be restricted and restrained.* If the fetus had an evil inclination it would rebel against being restrained in the womb, and leave the womb to certain death. Better to die than to be confined.

We all have an evil inclination that seeks to be free to do whatever it wishes, regardless what the consequences may be. I said to Sister O., "Your vow of obedience is a stress you will have to cope with all your life."

I referred Sister to one of the psychologists on our team. She was in every way emotionally healthy, and the difficulty with obedience was really the only significant problem.

Sister did well in therapy, and her relationships in the convent improved greatly. I met her several months later, and she said that she had no difficulty with obedience. "To be truthful," she said, "all I really needed to know was where my defiance was coming from. I can still bristle with anger sometimes when I am ordered to do something, but I say very softly, 'Anna (the stepmother), why don't you just go jump in a lake?' Then I laugh it off."

29
CHALLENGE OF FAITH I

Our group would meet weekly to review the cases we were working with and to deal with questions the staff might wish to present to Father Moylan.

At one such meeting, Father Moylan said, "I'm having some difficulty with a nun who is complaining that she has lost her faith. She is depressed about this, because it brings her whole life-commitment into question. I've seen her for three sessions, but I'm not making any progress. Does anyone have any ideas how I should proceed?"

I could not restrain myself from laughing. I said to Father Moylan, "The bishop had us put this group together because he was concerned that the average psychiatrist might attack the nuns' belief, and he wanted therapists who would be neutral toward religion. But now you're asking us to help make a nun *more* religious. That is a 180-degree switch."

"Yes, I understand," Father Moylan said, "but still, if one of you saw her, you might be able to guide me on how to help her." I agreed to see this nun for an evaluation.

Sister Z. was a twenty-nine-year-old woman. As she sat down in my office, she began crying. "I don't know what it is with me," she said. "Maybe I'm losing my mind.

"I haven't told Father Moylan this, but whenever I say the L-rd's name, I get an inappropriate thought. I feel so guilty that this is blasphemous and terribly sinful. It's crazy. It goes against everything I believe. I haven't been able to pray for fear of these ugly thoughts occurring."

Sister said that these thoughts began about six months ago. "I try to drive them out of my mind, but it's no use. As soon as I pronounce the L-rd's name, this terribly vile word jumps into my mind. How can I be a nun if I can't even pray?"

It was clear to me that Sister had OCD (obsessive–compulsive disorder). A person with OCD may have repetitious intrusive thoughts, often of a derogatory nature, or feel compelled to go through irrational ritualistic acts, or both. Sister did not have any compulsive rituals, just the objectionable intrusive thoughts.

I told Sister that I believe that OCD is primarily a physiologic disease, related to depression and panic attacks. Something has gone awry in the body chemistry so that the brain is stimulated to produce objectionable thoughts. Attempting to drive such unwanted thoughts out of one's mind can be counterproductive, similar to pushing down on a coiled spring, which only increases its force to jump back.

I told Sister that inasmuch as this was due to some physical quirk, she had no control over this. Hence, it was not blasphemous or sinful. But OCD is often referred to as the "doubting disease," because a person cannot accept reassurance. There is always a nagging "but what if?" Assuring Sister that she was not in sin would therefore be of little help.

"This condition can be treated effectively," I said. "My preference is to begin with medication, then add psychotherapy. In the meantime, continue to pray even if the thoughts occur.

Don't worry about this being sinful. G-d understands your condition." I told Sister I would prescribe her medication and check her weekly to regulate it, and I would refer her to one of the staff psychologists for therapy.

At the end of the third week, Sister felt much better. The obnoxious thoughts were infrequent, and she felt hopeful. By the sixth week, she was totally free of the troublesome thoughts, and continued therapy for several more months. At the end of a year, I weaned her off the medication, and advised her that if she had a recurrence, she should consult a doctor for the medication. Three years later, Sister was symptom free.

Father Moylan said, "No wonder I couldn't help her. I was talking religion, but her problem was physiologic."

30

CHALLENGE OF FAITH II

Father B. was a thirty-year-old priest who consulted me because he was unsure of his vocation, whether he should stay in the priesthood or leave. "I've discussed my concerns with my superiors. Of course, they are encouraging me to stay.

"My problem is not one of whether I can make the sacrifices that the priesthood requires, i.e., celibacy and poverty. Would I like to have a marriage relationship? Yes. Would I like to drive a Cadillac and have a summer home? Yes. But I gave this much thought before becoming a priest, and I decided I could handle them. Nothing has changed in that regard.

"The problem is that my motivation for becoming a priest and acceptance of the deprivations is, of course, contingent on a firm belief in G-d, and that's where my struggle is. The advice I am getting from my superiors is party line. Of course they weigh in on the side of belief, but I haven't been convinced. I often doubt whether G-d exists.

"I don't know how objective you can be, because as a rabbi, you too must toe the party line of belief in G-d. I'm looking for some psychological guidance. I can't consult the average psychologist, because many of them ascribe to Freud's opinion that all religion is neurotic."

I told Father that inasmuch as I am no longer a practicing rabbi, I really have little reason for preaching party line. In contrast to a practicing cleric, my professional career would not be affected if I did not believe in G-d. I also am free of any bias of keeping him in the priesthood.

I told Father that I didn't wish to enter into a theological discussion, knowing that he had certainly had an adequate dose of those. Nevertheless, my feeling was that the argument from design for the existence of G-d is irrefutable. It is only weak if one is ignorant of the complexity of the design of nature.

Just two brief examples. The movements of our eyes are controlled by six muscles on each eye. These twelve muscles must work in absolutely perfect coordination. The very slightest incoordination would result in seeing double. We move our eyes trillions of times in a lifetime. That we do not see double even once in a life span of eighty or more years attests to a degree of perfection and precision that could not possibly have evolved and had to be created by a super intelligence.

Another example is the pituitary gland, a pea-sized structure that lies at the base of the brain. It is the master control system of everything that goes on in the body, constantly analyzing the composition of the blood and issuing directives to many organs to keep the body chemistry stable. A four-story, fully computerized factory could not possibly do what this tiny gland does 24/7/365 for many decades. It is inconceivable that this came into being without design by G-d.

I think that the evidence for the existence of G-d is so overwhelming that doubting it can be due only to some powerful force that wishes to negate it. This powerful force is the body of desires that a person has, which can grossly distort one's judgment. The Bible says that a judge who accepts a bribe cannot possibly be objective. We are bribed by the many desires we have, and we are easily seduced to denying anything that is an obstacle to their achievement.

Belief in G-d is supra-rational. We use words such as "eternity" and "infinity," which are really meaningless, because we have no sense experience of anything eternal or infinite. Granted, belief in G-d requires a leap of faith, but the thought of the world not having been created by a superior being is even more irrational than belief in G-d.

I said to Father, "You may have miscalculated your willingness to accept the restrictions of priesthood, but rather than reconsider this, your mind has done a defensive maneuver and has you doubting the existence of G-d, which would, of course, make you leave the priesthood. But you don't have to rationalize a denial of G-d to achieve that.

"Therefore, I think your assertion that you are willing and able to accept the deprivations incident to priesthood needs to be carefully examined. If you wish, I can have one of our staff help you with this."

Father said he would give it some thought. He did not request a referral. I ran into him about a year later. He had left the priesthood. "You were right," he said. "I was fooling myself."

31
LET GO AND LET G-D

FATHER MOYLAN CALLED ME. "I DON'T know what to do about this case," he said. "This nun is preoccupied with something that happened fifty years ago and will not accept forgiveness for it. She just won't let go."

Sister Y. was a sixty-year-old woman who complained that for the past year she has been haunted for something she did in her childhood.

"This was in fourth grade," she said. "There was this girl, Brenda, who came from a well-to-do family. My family was poor. My father had abandoned the family when I was five, and my mother worked to keep us alive. Brenda came in the finest clothes, and her demeanor was that she was better than us because her father was rich. I was very sensitive to our poverty and I could not stand Brenda.

"One day I was overtaken by this evil impulse. Brenda had a pencil case that had pencils of all kinds of colors, erasers, a compass, a ruler, and whatnot. When she was out of the room and no one was looking, I took her pencil case and threw it away. At the time I didn't think I was doing anything wrong, and I was able to put it out of my mind. This past year, I began thinking of it, and I realize I had sinned by taking her pencil case. I have no way of apologizing to her, because I don't know where she is. I feel terrible about it. I've confessed it many times, and the priest told me to stop confessing it and go see a psychiatrist. So here I am."

Why would Sister develop this guilt feeling fifty years later? My initial thought was that she had developed a depression with OCD, and this recurring thought was a symptom of OCD. However, she had no other features of OCD, nor did she have other signs of depression. Getting to the root of this obsessive idea was going to be difficult.

Father Moylan's words, "She just won't let go," triggered in my mind the slogan of AA, "Let Go and Let G-d," and I decided to try to use it. I told Sister that I had an idea that would help her, but that she would have to follow my instructions even if they made no sense to her. I told her that I knew that she did not have an alcohol problem, but that I wanted her to go to AA meetings. She looked at me as if I had gone crazy. "What good would that do?" she asked.

"Trust me," I said.

I called Sister V., who was in recovery from alcoholism for several years. I asked her if she would take Sister Y. to some AA meetings. "She does not have an alcohol problem," I said, "but I want her to learn how to use 'Let Go and Let G-d.'" I wanted her to attend several AA meetings, and then to arrange a discussion meeting in which "Let Go and Let G-d" would be the theme.

Sister V. agreed. She met with Sister Y. and fortunately, they hit it off. Sister Y. found the meetings entertaining and did not object to attending them. She shared her obsessive thought with Sister V., who told her that when there is nothing one can possibly do about a problem, to turn it over to a Higher Power. "There is nothing you can do to make amends to Brenda, so turn it over to G-d. He will see to it that Brenda forgives you."

My whacky idea worked, and Sister Y. was relieved of her obsessive thought.

I have found that there is some kind of magic in the AA fellowship. The program works for many alcoholics who were not helped by psychiatrists. It is very difficult to let go of something that is nagging you, but if you share it with a number of other people who are "letting go and letting G-d," it is much easier to do so. Somehow, sharing the effort to let go with others enabled Sister to do so.

32

THE PAIN OF GROWTH

Sister D. had not yet made her final vows. She consulted me because she was in doubt as to whether she should indeed be a nun.

Sister said that her motivation in becoming a nun was to get away from a very uncomfortable home life. Her mother was very domineering. "I couldn't make a single decision for myself," she said. "She had to pass judgment on what I wore every day. Don't get me wrong. I love my mother, but she is an impossible person to live with. My poor father was also a victim of her tyranny. He could not stand up to her. I have two younger siblings. G-d help them. I don't know if I should stay or not. It's interesting that my vow of obedience doesn't bother me, and I respond to taking orders quite easily.

"Another thing is that I'm finding my spiritual growth painful. The demands on my personal life are hard to take. I know it will make me a better person, but it is nevertheless very uncomfortable. I don't know whether my motivation is strong enough to withstand the discomfort."

I think the dynamics of Sister's joining the convent is rather transparent. Her mother's domineering resulted in her intensely disliking her. I had an adolescent patient in the hospital who was relentless in railing against her mother. When she requested a weekend pass, I asked her why she wanted it. "I miss my mother," she said.

"But you've been telling me what a terrible person she is," I said.

"That's right," she said. "She's my mother, so I love her, but there's nothing about that woman that one can like." This young woman taught me that love and hate toward the same person can coexist.

I think that Sister was tormented by negative feelings toward her mother. Becoming a nun and taking a vow of obedience was making a statement: "I really don't hate her controlling me. I have willfully chosen to submit myself to domination by a woman. The Superior was a stand-in for her mother. Sister's subconscious mind engineered this defensive maneuver to eliminate the guilt of having hostile feelings toward her mother.

Sister complained of the pain engendered by spiritual demands. I told her that a lecturer asked the audience, "How many things have you learned from pleasurable experiences?" No one raised their hands. "How many things have you learned from unpleasant experiences?" A number of hands were raised.

I told Sister about what I had read in a magazine in a dentist's waiting room. The article was called "How Do Lobsters Grow?" Come to think of it, how *can* a lobster grow? It is encased in a rigid shell that does not expand.

The answer is that when the lobster grows, the shell becomes confining and oppressive. The lobster then retreats under a rock to be safe from predatory fish, sheds the shell, and produces a more spacious one. As the lobster continues to grow, the new shell eventually becomes oppressive, and the lobster repeats the process of shedding the confining shell and producing a larger shell. This process is repeated until it has reached its maximum growth.

So much for the article. Interesting, huh? But don't overlook the crucial point. The signal the lobster has that it's time to shed the shell is—*discomfort*. If lobsters had access to doctors, they might never grow. Why? Because when they felt the discomfort of the oppressive shell, they would get a prescription for a painkiller or a tranquilizer. With the discomfort gone, they would not shed the shell and produce a more spacious one. They would die as tiny little lobsters. For human beings, too, discomfort is often a signal that it's time to grow.

I felt that before making final vows, Sister should investigate the depth of her motivation for a religious life, and I arranged for her to see a therapist regularly. After six months in therapy, Sister decided in favor of being a nun.

33

HUMILITY

One Sunday morning I received a call from a sister. "Father Moylan gave us your number. I know you're not in the office Sunday, but we have a crisis with a young novitiate. Is it possible for you to see her now?"

"Of course," I said.

Sister K. was escorted to my office by two nuns. "We'll wait in the hospital lobby," they said.

When the door was closed behind them, Sister K. rushed over to my desk, took a paperweight, and hurled it on the floor. "I didn't come here to be treated like dirt!" she screamed. She then took some of the papers on my desk and threw them on the floor. "Now go ahead and call your guards to lock me up," she said.

"If you were throwing things at me, I might have had to call someone in self-defense," I said. "But as it is, you are telling me that you've been deeply hurt and you are very angry. If there is anything I can do to relieve the hurt, I'll try."

"At home I was treated like dirt," she said. "My older sister could never do any wrong, and my younger brother, a brat, was the prince. I was Cinderella. I couldn't take it. I joined the convent, where I would be someone people would respect. But I can't stand it here, and I can't go home. There's no place for me in this world," and she began sobbing uncontrollably.

I sat quietly by, and when the sobbing subsided a bit, I said, "Sister, I want you to sit back and take several deep breaths." As she calmed down a bit, I said, "If you feel up to it, you can tell me what happened that caused you so much pain."

Sister was silent for a few moments. Then she began speaking. "They told us that there was a nun visiting from out of town, and that she was a very holy person, and we novitiates would be privileged to have her talk to us. There were seven of us attending.

"This nun said that vanity is a terrible sin, and that although no one else may know we are vain, G-d knows what's in our hearts. We are told that we must be humble. "Humility is truth, and truth is humility," which means that we have to eliminate every vestige of vanity from our hearts and think of ourselves as nothing. She was looking right at me when she said it. She was telling me I have to be a nothing. Well, I was a nothing at home. I didn't have to come here to be treated as a nothing."

"I understand, Sister," I said, "but the nun may not have meant it the way it sounded to you. Do you think you can listen to me?"

"Okay," Sister K. said, "but should I pick up the papers from the floor first?"

"You can if you wish."

Sister gathered the papers and put them on the desk. "I'm sorry for what I did," she said.

"You are very young, Sister," I said, "and it takes a long time for us to bring our anger under control.

"I'm responding just to the fragmentary information you've given me. There is a rule that is as inviolable as the law of gravity, and I want you to remember it. It is that no one can put you down, except yourself. Regardless of what others may say or do, you should always have a sense of pride in yourself. That is not a violation of humility.

"It is unfortunate that you were treated badly by your family, and that caused you to be exquisitely sensitive. It is very much like having a prickly sunburn. Normally, if someone gives you a friendly tap on your shoulder, it can be pleasant. But if you have a bad sunburn, even a light touch can cause severe pain.

"The way you say you were treated at home caused you to have a very low self-esteem, and the nun's words touched this very sensitive area, causing you to feel deeply hurt."

"I guess you're right," Sister said. "But she was looking at me when she said it."

"There were only seven of you there," I said, "and I think she looked at everyone, but given your sensitivity, you felt that she was singling you out.

"I understand that you took a vow of humility. I know very little about Catholic doctrine, but I think that the concept of humility is very much like it is in the Jewish faith.

"Truth is the greatest virtue, and a person must know the truth about himself. To have a false self-concept is as sinful as any other falsehood. If you are bright, it is a sin to think that you are dull. If you are likable, then to think you are not likable is a sin. If you are gifted, then to think you are unendowed is a sin. Humility does not mean to think that you are inadequate. A person should know the truth about himself, but if one indeed has fine qualities, *one should not think that this makes him better than anyone else.* Vanity is thinking that you are superior to other people. Humility is to know the truth about oneself, but not think that this makes one superior to others. I think that the nun who spoke to your group would agree with me.

"I am a bit concerned," I said, "that your motivation to enter religious life was to get away from an abusive home. I think that this is something you should look into. I'm going to arrange for you to see a therapist on our team for some sessions, okay?"

Sister smiled. "Okay. But I feel so stupid for throwing a tantrum like a two-year-old."

"If you realize that regardless of how angry you get, you should avoid going into a rage, then this has been a very worthwhile experience," I said.

Sister followed up in therapy. She subsequently asked for a year's leave to reconsider her commitment to religious life.

34
THANK G-D I'M A PSYCHIATRIST

I RECEIVED A CALL FROM REVEREND JOHN, a Protestant minister. He had heard of our service to priests and nuns and wanted to see a psychiatrist. He did not feel comfortable in consulting a psychiatrist because "they consider religion a neurosis," and he did not want his religion challenged in therapy. Inasmuch as we serve priests and nuns, he felt he could trust us. However, since he is not a Catholic priest, he did not know whether we would accept him as a client.

Inasmuch as the diocese funded us to serve priests and nuns, I did not feel authorized to accept Reverend John. I called the diocese and they approved him.

Reverend John's suspicions of psychiatrists were really not justified. True, several decades ago, Freudian psychology dominated the field. Freud was an atheist, and he felt that all religion was pathological. Loyal psychoanalysts who worshipped Freud would indeed seek to "cure" people of their religious faith. However, the psychiatric/psychologic climate has changed significantly. While some of Freud's epochal contributions to the understanding of the human mind are valid, most therapists today do not consider religion to be a neurosis. There are many psychiatrists and psychologists that are religious.

Reverend John was thirty-eight years old, married, and the father of three children. Since childhood, he wanted to be a minister. His family was deeply religious, and his grandmother lulled him to sleep with religious stories and hymns. When he first called me he had been with his parish for six years, and felt he was well liked by his parishioners. Nevertheless, he was thinking of leaving the ministry.

I felt like disqualifying myself as a therapist for Reverend John. Having been a rabbi that left the rabbinate, I felt I could overidentify myself with him (this is called *countertransference*) and that I might not be objective. But I opened my desk drawer and decided I could work with him.

What has the desk drawer got to do with this? When I lecture to therapists, I warn them about the pitfall of countertransference, and I share a story with them.

There was a bookkeeper who was a perfectionist. Every day he came to work at exactly 7:55 a.m. and never left until after five. His work was meticulous. He had a ritual of unlocking his desk drawer when he came to work, nodding knowingly, then locking the drawer and attending to his books. This was a daily practice for thirty-five years. No one bothered to find out what the desk-drawer ritual was all about.

After thirty-five years, he retired. The next morning, all the other office staff gathered around the desk. They opened the drawer, which was empty, except for a sign in capital letters: THE DEBIT COLUMN IS THE ONE TOWARD THE WINDOWS.

I too have a card in my desk drawer. It reads: THE PATIENT IS THE ONE ON THE OTHER SIDE OF THE DESK. This reminder has helped me keep my personal hang-ups out of the therapeutic relationship.

Reverend John felt that he was at the breaking point, worn out, not sleeping well, and with little enthusiasm for his work. These symptoms can sometimes be due to a biochemical imbalance that can be treated with antidepressant medication. But I avoided jumping to a conclusion and listened.

Reverend John's predecessor, Reverend Burns, had served as pastor of the parish for forty years. The parishioners worshipped him, and his was a tough act to follow. (You may recall that I had a similar feeling when I visited a postoperative patient, who told me that when my father visited him, he was remarkably relieved of his pain, and this contributed to my leaving the rabbinate. So I opened my desk drawer and looked at my note.)

Reverend John felt chronically inadequate. Although he knew that this would be a problem for anyone in his position, it did not relieve his feelings of inadequacy.

Many people think of the minister, priest, or rabbi as representing G-d, and may have unrealistic expectations of him. Reverend Burns was indeed considered a Divine agent. The parishioners often would refer to their relationship with Reverend Burns. Although they had no intention of belittling Reverend John, he took it that way. He felt that they wanted him to be G-d-like.

Reverend Burns was available to the parishioners 24/7/365. They expected that they could call on Reverend John at any time and that he would respond, regardless of mealtimes or the late hours at night.

Reverend John's children were aged eleven, nine, and six. Matthew, the oldest, made it quite clear that he did not like to be a PK (preacher's kid). Reverend John had indeed told Matthew that the parishioners had expectations of him and that he did not have the leeway of lay people's children.

Reverend John's wife, Ethel, was a very private person who might be considered an introvert. Not only did she have to attend all the church's social functions, but she was expected to assist in organizing them. She felt that the parishioners expected immediate availability from her as well as from her husband, and was not too happy with this.

Reverend John had little time to devote to his family. He also had little time for himself. The parish was quite large, and there was no dearth of problems for which Reverend John's help was sought. He felt his family was being deprived of a husband and father. Yet, he felt well liked by the overwhelming majority of the parishioners, and he liked them as well.

What were his options? Resigning and finding another parish? Why should he think that a different parish would not have similar problems? Furthermore, he did like the work and he was very familiar with the parishioners. Breaking in a new relationship was not easy.

Should he leave the ministry and look for a different job? He had no qualifications for other work, and working as a salesman would be a financial loss for quite a while.

While the problems Reverend John presented were real, I felt that there were two factors that impaired his ability to cope with them: low self-esteem and burnout.

Reverend John had low self-esteem since childhood. Being put in a position where he succeeded a person the parishioners glorified aggravated the self-esteem problem. However, he was aware that he had qualities that Reverend Burns did not have, and he could provide for the parish in ways that Reverend Burns could not. It was important that Reverend John work on overcoming his low self-esteem.

I felt that Reverend John's depressive symptoms were manifestations of burnout. He had invested himself totally in the parish, neglecting other important aspects of life.

Just as we need adequate physical nutrition, we also need adequate emotional nutrition. The latter should come from our family, work, friends, recreation, and other interests. No single factor can provide 100 percent of one's emotional nutrition. If one has only a single source of emotional input, one is likely to develop burnout.

I think the term *burnout* is very apt.

On returning from yeshivah, my son told me about his resourceful roommate. Because of fire hazard, the boys in the dormitory were not permitted to have electrical appliances in the room. However, because they did their own laundry, they were permitted to have a clothes iron. What the roommate did was to turn the iron upside down, wedge the handle in a closed drawer, and eureka! He had a hot surface on which he could make coffee, popcorn, toast, or use as a griddle. What ingenuity!

But then, why do we need a number of different heat-producing appliances in the kitchen? Why not just use the clothes iron?

The heat of the clothes iron is produced by a delicate metal filament that turns red-hot when an electric current is passed through it. If the iron is used only for what it was intended, it has a normal life expectancy. If, however, in addition to ironing clothes, it is also used as a coffeemaker, toaster, popcorn maker, and griddle, the filament will burn out in a relatively short period of time. Why? Because it was not designed to carry the extra load of providing so many hours of heat. The delicate filament can't take it, and will soon burn out.

That is very often the reason for burnout. Everything in life has a purpose, and when anything is used for the purpose for which it was designed, it has a normal life expectancy. However, if you have unrealistic expectations of anything, making excessive demands of it and placing a greater burden on it than it was meant to carry, it will, like the element in the clothes iron, simply burn out.

Reverend John's emotional input was restricted to his parish work. He needed to spend more time with his family, and the parishioners would have to understand this. He also needed to cultivate other interests, whether hobbies, recreation, or study. As rewarding as the parish work was, it could not be expected to provide 100 percent of his needed emotional input. He needed input from additional sources.

I pointed out to Reverend John that he was overlooking something important. Much of today's youth is confused and without direction, which is why so many fall into the trap of drugs or other self-destructive behaviors.

When former First Lady Nancy Reagan launched her campaign to "Just say no to drugs," several researchers interviewed youngsters for their reaction. One fourteen-year-old girl said, "Why? What else is there?"

I told Reverend John that he had an excellent opportunity to enlighten the youngsters in his parish that there is more to life than getting high on drugs. Furthermore, Reverend Burns died two years before he took over, and Reverend John was there for six years. Youngsters aged fourteen to sixteen were just kids when Reverend Burns died, and had never developed the relationship with him that their parents had. With these youngsters, Reverend John could have a fresh start and did not have to feel that he was standing in Reverend Burns's shadow.

I suggested that Reverend John organize some group activities and studies for these youngsters. This would be a major contribution, and the youngsters' parents would be most grateful for the attention he was giving them.

I also suggested that Reverend John take some courses in marriage counseling, since these were problems for which his help was sought, and he needed to develop greater competence in this field.

I referred Reverend John to a therapist who could help him in these areas. He called me periodically, informing me that things were going very well for him.

I empathized with Reverend John. He is staying in the ministry, whereas I left it. Clients cannot barge into my home at their whim, and after-hours calls are taken by a message machine. People who want my services must make an appointment and cannot stop me on the street for curbside advice. Maybe I was a deserter by leaving the rabbinate, but I was glad I had made the decision to become a psychiatrist.

35
IGNORANCE OF ADDICTION

I HAD NOT PLANNED A CAREER as an addictionologist. It is not surprising that my training as a rabbi did not include information about addiction, but it is not understandable why in four years of medical school there was not a single lecture on alcoholism or drug addiction. Many of the symptoms that bring patients to a doctor's office can be due to alcoholism or drug addiction, but many doctors do not think of this possibility, and consequently miss the correct diagnosis, resulting in improper treatment. What is worse, many doctors unknowingly prescribe addictive tranquilizers, sleeping pills, and pain medication to addicts.

One would think that in psychiatric training, there would be great emphasis on substance abuse. After all, these chemicals have a marked effect on the brain, and it is absurd to try to treat someone for an emotional problem when one's thinking and feeling systems have been altered by chemicals. I wonder whether the subject was avoided because psychiatrists' patron saint, Sigmund Freud, was himself a cocaine addict.

My experience at St. Francis Hospital exposed me to alcoholism. Not having learned anything about this condition, I went to many meetings of Alcoholics Anonymous to get information from the horse's mouth. Who would know more about alcoholism than the people who had the problem?

It became evident to me that the thrust of the twelve-step program was not about alcohol or drugs, but rather character refinement. This was clearly stated by a recovering alcoholic on his twenty-fifth anniversary of sobriety. He began his talk by saying, "The man I once was, drank, and the man I once was will drink again." The twelve-step program enabled him to undergo a significant character transformation. I felt that although I did not drink or use drugs, I too could benefit from the twelve-step program, and I attended AA meetings regularly.

There are a number of twelve-step fellowships for people addicted to alcohol, drugs, food, sex, gambling, and spending. I found that some of the sisters who suffered from OCD (obsessive–compulsive disorder) benefited from the program Scrupulous Anonymous, which is very similar to the twelve-step programs. It is a Roman Catholic program, and may not be as effective for other faiths.

Attending AA made me aware that no one is immune to addiction. I treated many doctors, psychologists, lawyers, judges, athletes, and CEOs. Nevertheless, I was naive in thinking that priests and nuns were less likely than others to become alcoholics or drug addicts.

I was asked to see a nun who suffered from a convulsive disorder that was not responding well to treatment. Her neurologist thought that there may be some psychological problems complicating her condition. After several sessions, Sister finally admitted that she was addicted to Valium, and the convulsive seizures were due to withdrawal when she did not have enough of the drug. Sister had undergone tests—EEG, spinal tap, CT scan—because she had not revealed her drug use. She was subsequently treated for the addiction and has been free of seizures.

Another nun, Sister M.V., did not respond to treatment of depression by several psychiatrists. When she finally admitted that she was a heavy drinker, she was treated for her alcohol addiction, and the depression disappeared.

36

MISGUIDED KINDNESS

In 1981, I wrote a book entitled *Caution: Kindness Can Be Dangerous to the Alcoholic*, the theme of which was tough love. The alcoholic and addict vigorously refuse to discontinue use of the substance that gives them pleasure or relieves their misery. The only thing that will make the alcoholic or addict stop is hitting rock-bottom, that is, when the painful consequences of the addiction are greater than the pleasure it provides.

Family members or friends might come to the rescue of the addict, to try to relieve him/her of the misery incident to the addiction. They do this with every good intent, but are unaware that in doing so they are eliminating the only motivation that will make the addict seek treatment. This is referred to as "enabling," in that it actually enables the addict to continue the addiction.

For example, an alcoholic is arrested and imprisoned for drunk driving or for other offenses brought on by the addiction. The family may hire an attorney to get him out of jail, and may seek ways to get the charges dropped. They think they are doing the alcoholic a favor. While jail does not cure anything, it may help bring the alcoholic to his senses, especially if the court delivers a heavy punishment. Extricating the alcoholic from these unpleasant consequences enables him/her to continue drinking.

I was guilty of such misguided kindness. A priest was brought to the hospital for treatment of alcoholism. He was a very learned and prominent person in the church, and the diocese asked that I admit him to the general hospital, where he would be with "respectable" people, and not to the detox unit where he would be with drunks. I conceded to their wishes.

The nurses on the detox unit are very keen in observing the patient's behavior, and they can tell when he is going into withdrawal. The nurses in the general hospital lack this experience, and the priest's withdrawal symptoms were not noticed, resulting in its progressing to *delirium tremens*. When this was discovered, intensive treatment was instituted, but the patient died. I would have been much kinder to him had I insisted that he go to the unit with the other drunks.

This is why I insist that the family of the addict participate in Alcoholics Anonymous/Narcotics Anonymous family group meetings, because this is the only way they can learn what is truly helpful to the patient and avoid misguided kindness.

37

TOUCHLESS HUGGING

AT MEETINGS OF ALCOHOLICS ANONYMOUS, there is a great deal of hugging. I explained to the women that according to Torah law, I am not permitted to have any physical contact with any woman other than my wife and daughters. Therefore, I would wrap my arms around myself, hugging myself and saying, "Consider yourself hugged!"

When I entered the hall at a Gateway Rehab banquet, several of the St. Francis sisters were there, and they promptly hugged themselves. It occurred to me that whereas it is technically impossible to hug several hundred people, the symbolic "touchless" hug can be with everyone.

Someone sent me a rubber stamp with the figure of a little man hugging himself. It's a great way to give a hug through the mail.

There are two important messages conveyed in a touchless hug. First, it teaches that there can be a show of affection without physical contact. This is an important concept in an age where there is so much physical indulgence. It is important to remember that love is not dependent on physical contact.

A second message is delivered when one embraces oneself and conveys the message, "Consider yourself hugged." This is expressing the idea "I am embracing you just as I would myself." The biblical statement "Love your neighbor as you do yourself" implies that one indeed loves oneself. Loving oneself is a prerequisite for loving another.

In my book *Like Yourself and Others Will, Too*, I pointed out that the term "narcissistic personality" is a misnomer. This term is used to describe a person who appears to be in love with himself. He thinks he is always right and expects everyone to believe that. He demands to be catered to and to have his every wish fulfilled. He demands virtual universal adoration. He is grandiose, intolerant of others, and is easily offended. To all appearances, he is madly in love with himself.

The origin of the term is the Greek mythical figure Narcissus, who fell in love with himself when he saw his reflection in the still waters of a pond and discovered his own beauty. The fact, however, is that the narcissistic personality is someone who loathes himself because he has a terribly poor self-image, and his grandiose behavior is a desperate attempt to deny his self-disgust.

The narcissistic personality is extremely difficult to treat. If you frustrate any of his unrealistic demands, this intensifies his basic self-concept of inferiority, and his narcissistic behavior is intensified. However, if one yields to his demands, it just reinforces his behavior. It is a no-win situation.

A narcissistic personality cannot possibly have genuine love for another person. A person with a healthy self-esteem can love others and can be loved. This person is capable of fulfilling the biblical injunction "Love your neighbor as you do yourself."

38

THE FLYING NUN

THE FOLLOWING IS a personal account:

"I am writing this to share with you two very important aspects of my life. I am a sister, a Catholic nun, and I am an alcoholic. I used to believe, and many people actually do believe, that these two things can't ever go together in one person. They just don't fit; you must be either one or the other. In the process of recovery, those two aspects of my personality have become integrated and continue to be.

"Both my alcoholism and my membership in a religious community were part of a journey. The journey toward religious life passed a significant marker on the road when in 1979 at the age of thirty, I entered a convent. I'm not really sure why I made that decision at that time in my life. But it was always something that attracted me, and for some reason I had the freedom and grace to give it a try. This decision was to move me 650 miles away from my family and friends, and was pretty terrifying. It was like starting all over, yet I knew I had to give it a try. I just knew I'd never be happy if I kept putting off what I had a sense my heart was telling me.

"So against all odds, I made the big move from home to another city. Soon I was very homesick, missing my family and friends. I began to teach, and would come back and hang around the convent. There was tremendous loneliness much of the time because this was such unfamiliar territory. I hated that empty, lonely feeling but felt that in time it would pass as I adjusted. Actually, as the year progressed, I discovered that I really liked the sisters I was living with and found them welcoming and supportive. Yet I was very lonely. This was not in any way their fault, but mine. They tried to get close to me, but I would not let them.

"The other important aspect of my personality that I have come to recognize is that I am an alcoholic. I did not know that back in 1979 and 1980. It took a few years for it to become clear to me. For a while, I just chalked it up to adjustment. In the years that followed, however, it became apparent that I was in trouble, and that trouble had to do with my drinking. Living at home, I could justify my drinking to myself and others. I was in denial that there was a problem. An uncle of mine had died of alcoholism, and I was nothing like him. He was dirty, homeless, and would show up every now and then. Whenever he appeared, everyone got upset. No, I was nothing like him. I was a pretty heavy drinker in those days, and about once or twice a week I got quite drunk, but I was never caught driving drunk and never hurt anyone. I just had a lot of fun and it helped me unwind. I was clean, went to work every day, and was an excellent teacher.

"When I moved, all of the people, places, and things in my life changed. It was hard to cope. Here I was in a new city with no friends—it was a lot to adjust to. It was a whole new lifestyle for me, filled with strangers. I needed a best friend, and I found her in alcohol. (Hereafter, I will refer to alcohol as 'my friend,' because that is what it was. At least I felt at that time that alcohol was my friend, my best friend, my only friend.) Soon, I had become a daily closet drinker. Some days I drank openly, and other days I went off alone with 'my friend.' My 'best friend' began to take me away from the sisters because she warned me that they would not understand. She was right. Slowly, the drinking became more and more secretive, and I did it alone. She also convinced me that I could really relax with her, just like I used to back home. It worked for me then; why wouldn't it work now? She reassured me that I was okay and that this move hadn't been a mistake. She could help me adjust if I just relied on her, and slowly her power over me grew.

"Sometimes she took me places, but the next day I couldn't remember where. Sometimes I got really mad at her, and didn't want to go when she called, but she always managed to convince me that she was really helping with all of those feelings I had. Only she could really understand me.

"After a while she told me to steal money for her, and told me to lie and keep our relationship secret. I did all of that and just kept getting sicker and sicker. I was able to justify the stealing by telling myself that if these sisters knew so much about life, surely they would drink more and provide alcohol so that I wouldn't be forced to steal. They knew that I liked to have a few drinks every now and then. After all I had given up to join this community, the least they could do was to keep a supply of beer around. If they did that simple thing, I wouldn't have to go out so much. My 'friend' pointed out that if they really liked me so much, they'd do more to help me. So I relied on her more and more and removed myself from the sisters I lived with.

"When most people relate their drinking histories, they describe funny things that happened during this period. These things appear funny only in retrospect, but were either serious or disasters at the time they happened. I can't think of anything very funny that happened to me, except perhaps this. The only place I could hide in the convent to drink was the basement, but I needed an excuse for spending so much time there. What was my excuse? Why, I had to wash my clothes, of course. So I had stashed my beer in the basement, where I would wash my clothes, put them in the dryer, take them out of the dryer and put them back in the washer, then in the dryer again for several cycles. I'm not sure whether I was trying to fool myself or the other sisters, but that's what I did. The only redeeming feature of this craziness was that I had the cleanest clothes in the entire community.

"Needless to say, I went downhill fast. It was becoming apparent that I was in deep trouble. The only thing I could do was be honest and tell the sister in charge. I really wanted to do what was right; the lying and stealing had become too much for me and I could no longer keep it a secret. I didn't really tell her too much of what I was feeling, but I did tell her I thought I was an alcoholic. Much to my surprise, she didn't ask me to leave, but suggested I get help. I was so relieved that I began to feel like I had again entered safe territory, that things would be okay again. But what I did not realize was just how powerful my 'friend' was. I couldn't beat her alone, and things were not okay.

"Now that the secret was out, my 'friend' never let up on me. She kept me awake and was always after me. She constantly tricked me and whenever I let my guard down, she came after me, and I got drunk. I hated her and I hated me. I was trapped. If I was alone she took me. I was her prisoner and had no idea how to get free.

"Desperate for some kind of peace, I went to see a priest who was a drug and alcohol counselor in a city three hours away. He told me I was sick and talked to me about the disease I had. I felt so ashamed and had no real understanding of what was happening. Once a month, for the next year, I went to see him to try to deal with the alcoholism. But my 'friend' was always looking over my shoulder, telling me not to believe him. She tried to convince me that I was not like those people he talked about; I was stronger. She told me again that she was my 'best friend,' and that he was just trying to take me away from her.

"The priest suggested that I go to Alcoholics Anonymous (AA) once a week, and I initially tried that, but I couldn't keep it up. After all, people might recognize me there. What an embarrassment to my community. I felt it was better driving three hours to talk to him, and in that way, only he and my superior would have to know. My 'friend' came with me on every one of those rides, but I drank only on the way home. She helped me figure out what had gone on in the session and reminded me of how I could lie to keep us together.

"I soon became frustrated and told my superior that this trip to the priest was helping a little, but sometimes I still had to drink. She too suggested AA, and again I gave it a try. So, for the next year I went to AA meetings once a week. I sat in the back next to the only homeless man there. I focused on him and was able to block out what was being said. I was unaware of the forty or fifty other people in the room. After the meeting, I would buy a six-pack, go to a local park, and read the Big Book [the authoritative handbook of AA]. I did not understand it; in fact, I hated it. It seemed poorly written and the language was definitely not inclusive. There were a few stories about women, but not one about a nun, so I was sure this book was not for me. I went to the meetings, but no magic occurred. I was simply not getting drunk as often. And when I did drink, I'd feel really terrible because I had lost my capacity to hold alcohol. It made me sick a lot.

"Even though my drinking became very infrequent and months passed between episodes, I still felt trapped. I had no real peace, and out of fear, I decided to go into a rehab. I was pretty convinced it wouldn't help a lot, but I was too scared of hiding from my 'friend.' Maybe there she wouldn't find me. I had been hiding from her for nine months, but I knew it was only a matter of time before she found me. I could not hold on much longer. That's why I went to a rehab.

"I was admitted to the rehab as Sister Sue, but they immediately dropped the 'Sister,' because it was not important. I was just like the rest of the drunks there. I was both insulted and relieved. I listened and I learned. They told me what to do and I did it. I found G-d, I found friends, and I found a community I had always longed for. I entered the community of AA and it saved my life.

"Four years later, I found myself making my final vows before several hundred people. On that day I was able to do what I had learned to do privately each day at the rehab: get on my knees before G-d and ask for help to make it through the day. And every day since, I am able to take what has become a familiar position before G-d and offer Him the life He gave back to me just a few years before."

39

MEDICAL ADDICTION: A NUN'S STORY

Here is another personal account:

"Ever since I was a child, I remember complaining of stomach pain. In my adolescence, I was diagnosed with a peptic ulcer and treated for it. Nevertheless, at age twenty-four, I hemorrhaged and underwent surgery. I had much postoperative pain, which was treated with narcotic painkillers. I had received blood transfusions and developed serum hepatitis, which caused a severe depression. The depression greatly aggravated the pain, and I needed increasing doses of narcotics to control it.

"The doctor prescribed a thirty-day supply, one tablet to be taken every six hours. However, sometimes the effect wore off earlier, and I had to take an extra dose. I ran out of medication before the thirty days were up, and I called the doctor for a refill. 'I'll do it this time,' he said, 'but if you take it as prescribed, it will last thirty days. I will not give you another prescription before thirty days.'

"What was I to do? The pain was unbearable and my doctor did not understand how much I was suffering. I knew some of the sisters were prescribed pain medication, so I helped myself to some of theirs. I could not keep this up, because they would notice that their pills were missing.

"I had been the driver for the convent, and I knew which sisters went to which doctors, what medication they got, and what drugstores they went to. So I called the drugstore and said I was Dr. S.'s nurse, and ordered a refill of pain pills for Sister B., then went to the drugstore and picked it up. Since there were several doctors, I was able to keep this up for a number of months.

"But then the inevitable happened. Dr. S. prescribed a refill for Sister B., and the pharmacist said, 'But Sister B. just had a refill yesterday.' The doctor said he had not prescribed it yesterday, and the pharmacist became suspicious. Obviously, he checked other refills, and my game was discovered.

"The pharmacist knew who I was. I received a visitor who identified himself as a narcotics bureau agent. 'Sister,' he said, 'you have been calling in unauthorized prescriptions and picking them up for yourself. That is a federal crime. You are obviously addicted to narcotics, and I'm going to give you the opportunity to get treated in a rehabilitation facility.'

"I said, 'I'm not a junkie. I have severe pain and I need medication in order to survive. My doctor doesn't understand this. I don't need a rehabilitation facility. Tell my doctor to give me what I need.'

"The agent said, 'I believe you have pain, Sister, but you are an addict nonetheless.' He took out a paper from his pocket. 'You have committed a federal offense. This is a warrant for your arrest. If you enter a rehab program, I won't serve you with these papers. It's either a rehab or jail. It's as simple as that.'

"I broke down crying. The agent said, 'I've taken the liberty of arranging your admission to the rehabilitation program. I'll wait for you while you get your things together and drive you there. That way, I will not have to arrest you.'

"That was the darkest day of my life. Nobody understood me.

The rehabilitation program would take me off my medication, and I would suffer terrible pain. I wished I could just die.

"I was admitted to the detox unit. The nurses were very pleasant. One nurse said, 'We are going to reduce your medication gradually. You will have some pain. That can't be avoided, but we'll do everything possible to minimize your discomfort.'

"I met with the detox doctor and told him, 'I'm not a junkie. I'm a nun, and I needed the medication to control my pain, but my doctor did not believe me.'

"The detox doctor said, 'I believe you have pain, Sister, but here's what you must understand.'

"'The human body is very clever. The effect of the narcotic is very calming, and the body likes that effect. Therefore, the body produces pain in order to get more narcotic. You are not imagining the pain. It is real, but you must understand that your body has become addicted, and there is no end point to the amount of medication it wants.'

"I began feeling pain and complained to the nurses. 'It is still two hours before your next dose,' they said. The nurse called over one of the other patients in detox to sit with me. She was a wonderful woman who had become depressed when her husband left her, and she turned to alcohol for relief. There was a street junkie who was addicted to heroin. He sat with me as did several other patients. Finally, there were people who understood I was in pain. These people were most helpful in my weathering the detox.

"After I had been withdrawn from the medication, I joined the therapy group. I was still in pain but had learned to bear it.

"But oh, the group was terrible. They were all street junkies and alcoholics. And the language they used. Here I am, a nun, listening to terrible words. They told their stories, and described the things they did in their lifetime. I was dumbfounded. I just sat there and listened.

"The group leader tried to draw me into the conversation, but all I could tell them was that I was trapped into taking narcotics by physical pain. Eventually I came to realize that I was a criminal. I stole medication from other sisters who needed it. It took all my courage to admit to the group what I had done, but they did not condemn me.

"I had private sessions with a therapist and became aware of many things that had been bothering me and that I had just dismissed from my mind. I became aware that I had repressed many painful experiences, and that these had contributed to my seeking the relief from emotional pain. In fact, it was the emotional pain rather than the physical pain that was driving the addiction.

"I was in the rehab program for a total of three months, following which I attended meetings of Narcotics Anonymous regularly. Although most of the people there are street junkies, I no longer think of myself as better than them. I became known as the 'the sister junkie,' which was okay with me.

"It is now three years since I took my last pain pill. I sometimes still get pain, but I realize that it is the emotional pain that fires the physical pain. I have many numbers of people to call, and the support I get is unbelievable.

"The thought of being considered an addict was once intolerable. Now I smile at being called 'the sister junkie.'"

40
A PRIEST'S STORY

CAN A RECOVERING ALCOHOLIC GO BACK to social drinking again, assuming that he/she was a social drinker before the addiction developed? The overwhelming consensus among therapists who have worked with alcoholics or other chemical-dependent people is that one cannot return to "safe" drinking again. One alcoholic said, "Once a cucumber becomes a pickle, it does not ever go back to being a cucumber again."

Years ago there was a study that claimed that a certain percentage of alcoholics could go back to safe, controlled drinking. The percentage is irrelevant. Even it were one half of 1 percent, every alcoholic who wanted to drink again promptly seized upon this information to justify his use of alcohol: "I'm from that minority." Several years later there was a follow-up report by the same research group that stated their conclusions were premature. Those alcoholics who assumed that they could drink responsibly had again deteriorated into uncontrolled drinking.

So what does it mean if a person with an alcohol problem has been dry for a year or two? It means only that he has been dry for a year or two, and this should not be misconstrued to mean that the alcohol problem has been cured. People who have had a problem with alcohol should abstain indefinitely. Furthermore, since cross-addiction is a fact of life, they should also avoid use of any other recreational drug. In the event that they must receive an addictive-type drug as part of medical treatment, they must take great precautions to avoid a full-blown relapse.

Nothing illustrates the fallacy of a return to safe drinking as well as the following account by a priest who is in recovery:

"Both of my parents were born in Ireland. My father was for all practical purposes a teetotaler and my mother was abstemious. Our Roman Catholic faith was very important, and it was the center of our family life. I owe my vocation to the priesthood to several individuals, but if I made a list of them my parents would be at the top.

"I had no problem with alcohol during high school, college, or the seminary. When I first came to the fellowship of Alcoholics Anonymous, I used to say that I could not recall having any problems with drinking until my mid-fifties, but I now realize that my drinking was not normal even during the first year after my ordination.

"I was ordained in 1950 and was assigned to the pastor (there were three of us) in a middle-class parish in the northern section of Queens, New York. Almost every parishioner was a home owner. No one was wealthy, but we had very few indigent people in the parish. It was a great place, and the people were warm, friendly, and involved in parish life.

"After about five years there, my problem drinking became noticeable to my family and to some of the parishioners. A few reported their concerns to the pastor, who spoke to me about it. I denied that there was a problem and I thanked him for his concern. Actually I was very angry at the parishioners and at him.

"During this five-year period my priest friends had also become concerned about my drinking. I was the one who could not find my car or who had to be driven home after clerical gatherings. When the pastor first spoke to me I determined that I would never drink again. I kept that promise for about two years, acquiring the reputation of someone who had solved his problem.

"After this dry period I began to drink again—only a glass of wine at a meal now and then. No problem—so the drinking increased until the pastor and I had another little talk. Again I stopped, but this time the dry period lasted only about a year and a half. The next time it lasted a year, then six months. The nondrinking periods were getting shorter and shorter, and I had also become a closet drinker.

At the time of my tenth anniversary of ordination, the pastor asked the bishop to transfer me to another parish. I left and took up my new assignment determined that I would never drink again. My determination lasted two years. The next period of nondrinking lasted about eighteen months, then a year, then six months. Although these dry periods were similar to the ones already described, I was not able to see any kind of pattern developing, but it is very clear to me now.

At the end of an eight-year assignment in this second parish, the secretary for personnel called me and said the bishop wanted me to cover a situation in Queens where the pastor was drinking. I received this call during one of my dry periods, and because my drinking was now secret and periodic, everyone at the diocesan level thought I had solved my problem—so what better person than a recovered drunk to send to the drinking pastor in Queens?

I arrived at this parish, and within two months I'd gotten the pastor into treatment for his alcoholism. After a month at this treatment center, he returned to the parish on a Tuesday and by Wednesday he was a fall-down drunk. When he sobered up he told me that he wanted to resign as pastor and return to be chaplain in the hospital where he had worked before. He did so, and I was appointed pastor.

"I didn't touch a drink for two years. Then I began having some wine at meals. Well, you know the pattern that developed: the dry periods got shorter and shorter. I was able to keep it from most of the parishioners, because I was now the pastor and could go off for a few days to detox and leave my associate in charge. He had to be let in on my terrible secret, of course, and he was a very unhappy young man but went along with this for a while.

"One Saturday night when I went searching for him to say the seven o'clock Mass in my place because I was in no shape to appear in church, I could not find him. He knew I was drinking and he suspected that I might ask, so he just got lost. It was the best thing he could have done for me. Needless to say, the Mass was a disaster.

"After Mass I packed a bag and ran off to one of the hotels near JFK Airport. When I got to the hotel I called my secretary and let her know where I was. I was left alone all day Sunday while I 'tapered off' on beer at the hotel bar. On Monday morning my associate called and made two demands of me. He insisted that I get medical help, and that I enter AA. I agreed, but I didn't plan to be at the hotel when he arrived to take me wherever he wanted to take me.

"He was wise enough to know that I would probably run out on him, so he had another priest on the road a few minutes away from the hotel when he made his call to me. I was trapped. I was taken to a program in Manhattan and to Cabrini Hospital's detox unit.

"It seemed to take forever to be admitted to the hospital. I was in very bad physical shape because I was at the beginning of the withdrawal process. I suggested to the priest who had driven me to the hospital that he could leave now because I could certainly take care of myself. Thank G-d, he did not leave; he must have known that given half a chance I would dash out to the nearest bar. I finally got up to my room and was feeling as low as I have ever felt in my life, when one of the orderlies asked me if I was ready to attend my first AA meeting. I thought I was in no shape to attend anything but my wake! However, I thought and I believe this was a great grace from G-d, that if this was what I would have to do to get sober, then this was what I would do.

"As the years passed in the fellowship of AA, I gradually began to realize that my problem was that I could not handle success. I never seemed to turn to the bottle when I was faced with a problem; I turned to the bottle only to reward myself after I had coped with the problem. This was certainly true in my second and third (final) assignments. It took about two years in my second assignment to feel comfortable with the new parishioners and with the programs I was attempting to run for them. As soon as I felt at home and saw some good results in my work, I rewarded myself with a glass of wine at dinner.

"In my third assignment I discovered that it took me about two years to feel comfortable in the place and with the work, and again I rewarded myself with a little wine at dinner. I also realize today that the amount of wine I took when saying Mass was much more than I should have taken. It became my morning drink, and as time went on, it became the spark to the fuse of my addiction.

"I will always be grateful to my associate for having the courage to stand up to me and make those two demands of me. I have never for one moment been tempted to drink since I entered that detox ward in lower Manhattan. I have only one very minor regret: When I drank, I wanted to drink as a gentleman, but because I am a victim of an insidious and fatal disease, I drank only as a drunk. It is, as I've said, a very minor regret."

41

WAYWARD PRIEST

FATHER M., A MAN OF THIRTY-EIGHT, consulted me. He had been a periodic alcoholic who could go for months without a drink, but if he took a drink, he ended up intoxicated. The diocese of his hometown transferred him to Pittsburgh, and he was not permitted to return home.

At the time I saw him, he was actively involved in Alcoholics Anonymous and was sober more than three years. He asked whether there was any way we could intervene so that he could visit his elderly mother, whom he had not seen for several years.

I suggested the program that is used for physicians who recover from alcoholism or drug addiction. Many are highly skilled and could give years of valuable service, but strict steps must be put in place to protect the public in the event of a relapse.

The plan requires close monitoring. In addition to active involvement in AA or NA, the doctor must have a therapist. He is subject to random blood or urine tests. The therapist may call him at any time, and he must promptly go to the designated laboratory for tests. If he does not show up within eight hours of the call, it will be assumed that he had a relapse and will not be allowed to practice medicine. The therapist may call him to be tested on two consecutive days or weeks apart. He has no knowledge about when he can expect a call. This monitoring must continue for at least two or three years, and may be extended by the therapist. The therapist submits regular progress reports to the State Physician Health Program.

I suggested to Father M.'s hometown diocese that a similar plan be adopted for him, stipulating that he would have to sign a contract that included the therapist's right to notify the diocese of any breach in behavior or noncompliance. The diocese agreed to this plan and assigned someone to whom the therapist was to report. Father M. was permitted to visit his mother at six-month intervals.

Father M. was extremely grateful for our help. I met him at AA meetings, and the last time I met him he was eight years sober.

42

THERE IS NO IMMUNITY

WHY DO NUNS AND PRIESTS BECOME addicted to alcohol or other chemicals? *Because they are human beings.* Strange, no one asks why do nuns and priests become diabetic or develop asthma. This is because these conditions are diseases that can affect anyone. Alcoholism and drug addiction, however, are not thought of as diseases but as moral failures, and therefore, devoutly religious people are expected not to have these conditions.

But why is alcoholism a disease? After all, the person himself lifts the drink to his mouth. A bit of understanding is necessary.

In our culture, the social use of alcohol is widespread. The media encourages sports fans to drink beer. I don't know of anyone who will condemn a person for having a beer. Most social events at which food is served—weddings, graduation parties, office holiday parties, and so on—all feature alcohol, and no one thinks there is anything wrong with having a drink. The fact is that there is nothing wrong with judicious use of alcohol. However, there are some people who react abnormally to alcohol, almost like an allergic reaction, which does not affect everyone.

The problem is that there is something in the brain of the alcoholic that causes two things: (1) a craving for alcohol that can be very intense, and (2) *a blocking out of the awareness that there is anything wrong with how he is drinking.* Everybody can see the ruinous effects that alcohol has on the person—everyone, except the alcoholic. Whatever is going on in the alcoholic's brain *blinds him to his problem.*

We do not know what it is that is different in the brain of the alcoholic and what causes the difference. Inasmuch as alcoholism does run in families, there is probably a genetic factor.

So in our society, we cannot fault a person for taking a drink, and if he has this quirk in his brain that causes him to crave alcohol and blinds him to what the alcohol is doing to him, we cannot condemn him for that either.

What about drug addiction? Isn't a person responsible for taking the first illegal drug?

First of all, the number of people who are addicted to legal drugs is probably greater than the number of cocaine and heroin addicts. Some doctors write prescriptions for tranquilizers, sleeping pills, and pain medication very liberally, without awareness of their addictive nature. The same kind of quirk in the brain that causes alcoholics to crave and be oblivious to their problem causes the drug addict to be likewise

Some patients may use heavy narcotics for pain control, and when the medical problem is cured, they do not continue the use of the medication. Others, even with lesser use, may become addicted. The quirk in the brain may actually cause physical pain, for which the person may use narcotics.

Youngsters are indeed very foolish for experimenting with drugs. Sometimes, out of curiosity, they will use their parents' sleeping or pain medication. Sometimes they are offered a pill by a friend, and if they are vulnerable to addiction, they will continue using it, oblivious that they are becoming addicted.

Let us not forget that many people think that marijuana is safe. This is not true, but it has been estimated that more than 50 percent of college students use marijuana with some frequency.

All these factors apply to priests and nuns as well. Hence, it is not a moral failure, unless you consider picking up the first drink a moral failure.

Denial of the problem is common to all alcoholics and addicts. The denial is even greater among people who feel that their reputation is at stake. Priests and nuns are afraid of the stigma of alcoholism and drug addiction, and are desperate to keep it secret. Unfortunately, this prevents them from getting help early in the course of the addiction.

43

A COMMITTEE PLAN

BECAUSE OF MY EXPERIENCE in treating alcoholism and drug addiction, I was appointed to the governor's committee on the problem, which entailed making periodic trips to the state capital, Harrisburg. At one meeting, a plan of action was proposed, which was the typical kind of thing a committee would do. I was asked for my opinion on the plan, and I responded with a story of the wise men of Chelm. These stories are about a group of villagers who were remarkably foolish in a quaint sort of way.

ONE MORNING, the people of Chelm awoke to find that there had been a snowfall overnight, and the town was covered with a carpet of pristine snow, a beautiful sight to behold. The townsfolk realized that the beadle of the synagogue, who makes early morning rounds to corral the worshippers to services, would be trampling the beautiful snow with his feet. What to do?

A committee was quickly convened to deal with the problem. After much deliberation, the committee decided that in order to prevent the beadle from ruining the snow, *four people would carry the beadle from house to house.*

"That's my opinion of your proposal," I said.

44

THE SELF-ESTEEM ISSUE

One day, two sisters approached me asking whether they could have several group meetings on issues common to many of the nuns. It sounded like a good idea. The word spread, and about twenty nuns from several convents attended.

Before long, the issue of self-esteem came up. This was a subject that I had addressed in books and articles, not only because I believe it is crucial to mental health and well-being, but also because it was a problem I struggled with for years. Clinically, I found low self-esteem to be a factor in every psychological disorder, and sometimes the principle factor.

Let me define "low self-esteem." This refers to a person having a distorted self-concept, thinking himself to be much less than he in fact is. There are various feelings of inferiority and not being likable, and a lack of self-confidence. Although the person may be gifted and handsome, he does not see himself that way. Rather, one has a feeling of negativity which is in defiance of facts. There is the "paradox of low self-esteem," according to which people who are in fact superior may have a lower self-esteem than people who are not as well endowed.

I've found the low self-esteem problem to be extremely common, if not ubiquitous. The origin of low self-esteem is not clear. Certainly parental neglect or abuse can cause it, as can physical limitations and a variety of other deprivations. However, it can also occur in the absence of an identifiable cause. I had a wonderful childhood, loving parents and I excelled in many things, I graduated high school at sixteen with honors. Yet, I was haunted by feelings of inadequacy.

Perhaps the prevalence of low self-esteem is a consequence of civilization. A while back, several psychologists built an experimental house in dimensions for adults as the average house is for children, i.e., the ceilings were twenty-five feet high, the chairs and tables were three times their normal height, and the doorknobs were beyond reach. They had some perfectly normal people live in this house, and by the third day, they were showing symptoms of neurosis.

This is the environment in which our children live. Imagine if you had to climb to sit in a chair or reach the tabletop, or you had to stretch to reach a doorknob. To our children, the world is a reversal of Lilliput, the fictional island in *Gulliver's Travels* where the inhabitants were six inches tall. For our children, the world appears to be inhabited by a race of giants in which they feel insignificant. Perhaps in primitive tribes, where there were no doors to the huts and where one ate sitting on the floor, children did not feel so infinitesimally tiny.

Whatever the reason, many if not most people develop low self-esteem. This is a very distressing feeling, and they seek to cope with it in a variety of ways. One of my defenses was people pleasing. Because I wished to be liked but did not consider myself to be likable, I did things for people in the hope that I would get their affection. I was exquisitely sensitive to criticism. The slightest suggestion of disapproval sent me into a depression. I had no idea that these behaviors were my way of coping with my low self-esteem.

Underachievers and overachievers may both be the way they are as a result of low self-esteem. The underachiever fails to live up to his potential because of lack of self-confidence, and the overachiever tries to prove to the rest of the world as well as to himself that he is not inadequate.

During my third year at St. Francis Hospital, I went on a two-week vacation. My three years there were of unrelenting stress. On a good night, I was awoken by the emergency room four or five times, and on a bad night it could be ten times.

I told my wife that I did not want to do any sightseeing. I needed two weeks of perfect quiet. I would sit in an easy chair with the drapes closed and breathe. Perfect quiet.

We ended up in Hot Springs, Arkansas, whose industry is horse racing, which begins in February. We arrived in December, at which time the town was dead. All the stores were boarded up. Just what I needed.

Being that I suffered from back pain, I took advantage of the curative mineral baths there. I was let into a cubicle, with a tub full of hot water naturally heated in the earth. I entered the whirlpool bath and felt I was in paradise. No one could reach me, not a patient, nor doctor, nor nurse, nor social worker, nor lawyer—this was just what I had hoped for.

After about six minutes, when I arose to emerge from the tub, the attendant said, "Where are you going, sir?" I told him I was ready for the next step in treatment. "You can't go to treatment until you've stayed in the whirlpool for twenty-five minutes," the attendant said.

Not wishing to lose the treatment, I returned to the tub, but after five minutes I said, "I have to get out of here."

"If you leave now," the attendant said, "you lose the treatment." I returned to the tub, but the next fifteen minutes were pure torture.

That afternoon I had a rude awakening. I realized that I was able to take the constant stress and pressure at the hospital for three years, but I could not tolerate paradise for more than ten minutes. Something was wrong.

On my return home, I consulted a psychologist, who explained: "If you ask people how they relax, one person may say, 'By reading a good book.' Another may say, 'By going fishing.' Another might say, 'By doing needlework,' and another might say, 'By listening to music.' Each one is telling you what they *do* to relax. But true relaxation is doing nothing. These things are *diversions* rather than relaxation.

"In your whirlpool cubicle, you were deprived of all diversions. There was nothing to listen to, nothing to watch, nothing to do. Stripped of all diversions, you were left in immediate contact with yourself. No wonder you couldn't tolerate it. You don't like yourself, and it is difficult to be in intimate contact with someone you don't like."

What the psychologist said made sense. But what was there about me that I disliked so much that I could not stand myself? I embarked on a journey of self-discovery. It took years, but I am now free of the various defenses I used to cope with my low self-esteem. I have since been back to Hot Springs, and I enjoy the whirlpool for a full twenty-five minutes.

Virtually all of the nuns said that they think they have low self-esteem. We would discuss the subject in greater detail in several sessions. I suggested reading material on the problem, and if this did not resolve it, to consult a psychologist.

45

IDENTITY

THE DISCUSSION OF LOW SELF-ESTEEM led to the issue of identity. A person should have an identity of one's own, and not be dependent on other people to determine who he is. I pointed out that people who lack a true identity may try various things to give them an identity. To illustrate this point, I told the nuns one of my favorite folktales of the wise men of Chelm.

ONE DAY, a citizen of Chelm was at the public bathhouse. It suddenly dawned upon him that without clothes, most people look alike. He became quite anxious with the thought, "When it comes time to go home, how will I know which one is me?"

After pondering this a bit, he came up with a brilliant solution. He found a piece of red string and tied it around his big toe. He was now distinctly identifiable.

Unfortunately, in the process of sudsing and showering, the red string fell off his foot, and when another bather stepped on it, it stuck to his foot.

When it was time to leave, the first bather looked at his foot, and seeing nothing on it, was perplexed. Then he noticed the other man with the string on his foot. He approached him and said, "I know who you are, but can you tell me, who am I?"

SOME PEOPLE seek an identity by having the equivalent of a red string. Their identity is the luxury automobile in the driveway or the impressive facade on their mansion. But this is hardly an internal identity. What happens if one sells the car? Does the identity go along with it?

It is not much different if one's identity is "I am a doctor" or "I am a lawyer." That is a description of what one *does* rather than what one *is*. If one's only identity is "I am a doctor," then one shares an identity with myriads of other doctors, but one does not have an individual identity.

I should have been prepared for the reaction to this story. One nun asked, "Is the habit I wear my version of the red string?"

I fumbled for words. "There are good reasons that your religion has for wearing the habit, but it is possible that for someone it might be a way of getting an identity."

Well, the nun took back the message that "Dr. Twerski said we wear the habit to have an identity," and this caused quite a furor in the convents. I got a call from the bishop and explained what I had said. The bishop's response was to get a message to the convents to "listen to Dr. Twerski." As a result, the attendance at our sessions doubled.

46
SPIRITUALITY AND RELIGION

A NUN ONCE SAID TO ME, "I heard that you said that if a person is spiritual, he does not need religion. What is spirituality if not religion?"

I have often been misquoted, so this was just another instance. Of course, I never made such a statement, but it is important to define spirituality, because it is not the same thing as religion.

It is obvious that a human being is a composite creature, comprised of a body plus "something else." The body is essentially an animal body, with rather minor differences. The emotional drives that are indigenous to animals are present in humans as well. What makes us unique as human beings is that "something else," which consists of those human features that animals do not have.

Science has defined man as *homo sapiens*, thereby making *intelligence* the single distinguishing feature that separates man from animals. According to this, a person with multiple degrees and the most advanced intellect would then be the most perfect human being. It should be obvious that this is wrong. A highly educated person can be vulgar, selfish, cruel, and immoral—hardly what one would consider an ideal human being. The "something else" that gives human beings their uniqueness is more than just intellect.

In addition to greater intelligence, some of the more obvious uniquely human features are (1) the ability to learn from the history of past generations; (2) the ability to search for truth; (3) the ability to reflect on the purpose and goals of life; (4) the ability to have self-awareness; (5) the ability to volitionally improve oneself; (6) the ability to have perspective, to contemplate the future, and to think about the future consequences of one's actions; (7) the ability to be considerate of others and to be sensitive to their needs; (8) the ability to sacrifice one's comfort and possessions for the welfare of others; (9) the ability to empathize; (10) the ability to make moral and ethical choices in defiance of strong bodily drives and urges; (11) the ability to forgive; (12) the ability to aspire; and (13) the ability to delay gratification. I'm sure you can come up with many more traits that people have that are not present in animals in the wild.*

For example, animals in the wild are motivated by only one drive: self-gratification. Domesticated pets may adopt human traits, and dogs have been known to have true devotion to their masters. However, animals in the wild are not altruistic, nor do animals have a conscious sense of mission. The care of a mother for her young is a biological instinct rather than a sense of moral obligation, as is the herd instinct for self-preservation. To the best of my knowledge, an animal will not sacrifice its own comfort or well-being for the welfare of a strange animal.

---

* Abraham Twerski, *Happiness and the Human Spirit: The Spirituality of Becoming the Best You Can Be*, 2007. Permission granted by Jewish Lights Publishing, Woodstock, VT, www.jewishlights.com.

The ability to sacrifice one's comfort and possessions for the betterment of a total stranger is unique to man, and, therefore, defines man every bit as does *sapiens*.

I group all these features together and say that *the sum total of all the traits that are unique to humans is what we may refer to as the human "spirit."* As you can see, there are no frankly religious elements in this definition. One may certainly add a religious dimension to the spirit, but even an agnostic cannot deny that these are uniquely human features.

As noted, all these features are uniquely human *abilities*. For example, a person may or may not reflect on the purpose of his existence, but every human being has the *ability* to do so. If one exercises and implements these elements of the spirit, then one is being *spiritual*. Spirituality can therefore be thought of as *being the best human being one can be*.

Where does religion come in?

One of the uniquely human traits that comprise the human spirit is "the ability to reflect on the purpose and goals of life." Note that implementation of this trait is not necessarily *finding* a goal or purpose. Rather, it is the *contemplation of and search for* a goal and purpose that makes one spiritual.

In our daily lives, we have myriads of intermediate goals. The goal of driving into a gas station is to refuel, and the goal of driving to the office is to get our work done so that we may earn a livelihood, which in turn has a goal of supporting the family. But what is the ultimate goal of one's life?

One might say that "being the best person one can be" is an ultimate goal. This may not be satisfactory to a religionist, who may ask, "What is the purpose of being the best person one can be?" Or, if one has an ultimate goal of doing something for the betterment of mankind, one may ask, "What is the purpose of mankind?"

There is an anecdote of two vagrants who were arrested for loitering and brought before a judge. The judge asked the first vagrant, "What were you doing when the officer arrested you?"

"Nothing," the vagrant answered.

The judge then turned to the second vagrant, "And what were you doing when you were arrested?"

The man pointed toward his buddy. "I was helping him," he said.

It is obvious that if one is helping someone who is doing nothing, one is doing nothing oneself.

Nonreligionists may say that actions that are not self-centered are uniquely human and are indeed much finer than self-centered behavior, yet one may ask, "What is *their* ultimate purpose?" If the universe was not designed by an intelligent being for a specific purpose, but just "happened" to come about as a result of a freak accident that converted primordial energy into matter, which over billions of years evolved into life on the planet Earth, then the world as a whole has no specific purpose for its existence. Therefore, there can be no ultimate purpose to the existence of mankind. It is rather meaningless to seek an ultimate goal and purpose for oneself if the entire universe is purposeless.

One who believes that G-d created the world for a specific purpose known only to Him, and via revelation or through prophets instructed humans to live in a way that this purpose would be fulfilled, can have an ultimate purpose. Inasmuch as the concept of G-d involves attributes such as infinity, eternity, omniscience, and omnipresence, qualities with which humans have never had any sensory experience, it is a suprarational concept. All claims to prove the existence of G-d logically are subject to argument, and in the final analysis, belief in G-d requires a leap of faith. Indeed, natural disasters such as tsunamis, earthquakes, tornadoes, hurricanes, and incurable disease of both children and adults defy any logical explanation of why a benevolent G-d would allow these to occur. A believer must go beyond logic, and this is the leap of faith. The person that has traversed this leap and has a firm conviction in G-d as the Creator of the universe can reason to an ultimate purpose in his existence.

Thus, one can be spiritual even though one is not religious, but when one tries to implement one's ability to focus on a purpose in life, one is stymied.

Belief in Creation is also essential for self-esteem. To "esteem" something is to value it. Why do things have value for us? Essentially for one of two reasons: (1) they serve a purpose, or (2) they are ornamental. If my beautiful grandfather clock stops working, I keep it for aesthetic reasons; it is a handsome piece of furniture. When my can opener goes dull, I throw it away. Since it cannot function and is not decorative, it has no value.

What gives me value? Very few people are so handsome as to be decorative, and even they may lose this beauty as they age. My value is in my function. If I don't have an ultimate goal, what value can I have? Without feeling one has value, one cannot have self-esteem.

So one can try to be spiritual without being religious, but one important aspect of spirituality—working toward an ultimate goal—cannot be met.

Following the discussion on spirituality, a young woman, a novitiate, consulted me. "I think I understand something," she said. "One can be religious even if one is not spiritual.

"There is one older sister I cannot stand. She is mean to me. True, I'm only a novitiate and she has been in the order for more than thirty years. But does that give her the right to criticize everything I do? Some of the other sisters feel the same way about her. She bosses everyone around, and everyone is afraid to stand up to her. She may be religious, but she is not a spiritual person."

I told Sister that there are people who are control freaks, and they exist in the convents as well as in the lay population. I believe that many control freaks are people with low self-esteem, and that domineering others gives them a sense of being somebody. I told her that there are books on how to best relate to a control freak.

Sister said, "I'm especially sensitive to this. My older sister is a control freak, and one of the reasons for my becoming a nun was to get away from her."

I told Sister that she should consult Father Moylan. The choice of a religious life in order to escape an unpleasant family situation is not wise, and unless there are positive reasons for being a nun, this motivation may be inadequate to provide a happy adjustment.

Father Moylan recommended that Sister go into therapy to investigate her motivation. I saw her two years later, and she was happy with her choice of a religious life.

47
THE BIRTH OF GATEWAY

For some reason, Pittsburgh is not permitted, by charter, to have a public hospital similar to Bellevue in New York, Cook County Hospital in Chicago, or Philadelphia General Hospital. In cities with a public hospital, the private hospitals used to send the undesirables (alcoholics) to the public hospital. In Pittsburgh, which did not have a public hospital, they sent them to jail, where some died. The Sisters were appalled by this. (Sister Adele would always say, "That patient could be your father.") So St. Francis had an open admission policy for alcoholics.

It soon became evident to me that we were not accomplishing much with our alcohol detoxification unit, better known as the "drunk tank." Patients would stay a few days, get dried out, attend an in-house AA meeting, and leave. Some 95 percent never followed up with attendance at Alcoholics Anonymous meetings. Occasionally, we would send an alcoholic to a rehabilitation facility near Philadelphia. This did not allow for continuity of care.

I told Sister Adele that we were not treating alcoholics adequately, and that we needed a rehab facility in Pittsburgh where an alcoholic could spend several weeks after detoxification and at least get a start on sobriety. Sister agreed and told me to go ahead with developing a rehab center.

Neither Sister Adele nor I had any concept of reality. How would a rehab support itself when insurance did not cover treatment for alcoholism? There were meager state funds that covered only 70 percent of cost for selected patients. But ignoring reality, I formed a committee of interested citizens and proceeded to solicit start-up funds from charitable foundations and industries. We secured a mortgage, underwritten by the Department of Housing and Urban Development, and erected a $2.5 million, one-hundred-bed facility.

Gateway Rehabilitation Center. Note sign in the foreground.

Gateway admitted its first patient in January 1972, and the first trickle of insurance coverage did not occur until August 1975. I kept Gateway alive by passing the hat. Finally, I had exhausted my welcome and could not raise any more money.

Sister G., then the CEO of Gateway, called me. "We can't meet next week's payroll," she said.

"Sister," I said, "I have no way of getting any money. If we can't meet next Thursday's payroll, we'll shut down Thursday, but not one day earlier. We tell our patients to live one day at a time, and that's what we will do too."

Thursday passed uneventfully. We remained open, but I didn't ask how. I just assumed it was another one of the miracles that people in AA talk about.

Years later, I discovered that our bookkeeper, who was a recovering alcoholic, took out a mortgage on his home to make the payroll. Talk about ignoring reality. He was seventy, and there was no prospect that we could ever repay him. Somehow we did, and Gateway progressed to be the vibrant institution it is now. With a network of outpatient clinics in Pennsylvania and Ohio, our staff sees hundreds of patients every day.

It is that kind of devotion of recovering alcoholics to others that need help that is the backbone of recovery.

48

A UNITED EFFORT

IN 1971, I RECEIVED A CALL from a local rabbi that he had been contacted by a family in Israel. Their child was born with a heart defect, and they were told that at age seven he should undergo corrective surgery. The family members were followers of the Chassidic rabbi, Rabbi Menachem Schneerson of Lubavitch, who advised them to have the surgery done in the United States, because at that time the technology there was superior. I contacted a pediatric heart surgeon, who said that he could perform the operation.

I raised funds to enable the family to come to the United States. The problem was that neither the child nor the parents knew a word of English, and there was no way that they could communicate with the hospital staff. I put out a call for all Hebrew-speaking people in Pittsburgh to contact me, and more than thirty people responded. We arranged a schedule such that each person would spend several hours with the family, and one volunteer would not leave until his/her relief came.

This effort resulted in a strong bond among all who participated. Although the surgery was uneventful, the tension of open-heart surgery was great, and the parents received much support from the interpreters. After the recovery period we had a going-away party for all participants. The surgeon waived his fee, and the hospital reduced the bill to a bare minimum.

Several years later, on a visit to Israel, I went to see the family. I could not see the child, who was away playing basketball. That he could be a healthy youngster capable of playing sports was a great reward. That the community could join ranks to provide the necessary support was equally great.

49

WHAT I LEARNED

THE PSALMIST SAYS, "From all my teachers I grew wise" (Psalms 119:99). The Talmud says, "Who is wise? He who learns from every person" (*Ethics of the Fathers* 4:1). In this wide world, we can learn from everyone and everything.

Rabbi Yisrael of Salant was once walking with several disciples when he saw a procession of three horse-drawn wagons loaded with hay. The middle horse was eating the hay from the wagon in front of him, and the third horse was eating from the middle wagon.

"What does that teach you?" Rabbi Yisrael asked his students. When there was no reply, he said, "The horse pulling the first wagon has nothing to eat, but he does benefit, because his load becomes lighter as the horse behind him eats. The load of the third horse does not become any lighter, but he can eat from the middle wagon. The middle horse has the greatest benefit, because he can eat from the wagon in front of him and his load becomes lighter as the horse behind him eats from his wagon.

"This teaches you that the greatest benefit is accrued by one who takes a middle-of-the-road approach and avoids either extreme."

If we keep an open mind, we can learn from things we see in the street, even from horses. I may not be wise, but I've been privileged to learn many things from many people.

I was fortunate in being exposed to people and things I could learn from, and this has substantially supplemented what I received from formal training, both as a psychiatric physician and as a rabbi.

Along with the masters of classic literature, I found profound psychological insights in the cartoons of Charles Schulz, creator of Snoopy and Charlie Brown. This resulted in my writing several books on Schulz's insights. I was also privileged to hear many stories from which I could derive valuable psychotherapeutic tools.

"G-d made man straight, but they [people] sought many calculations" (Ecclesiastes 7:29).

It is well known that some people derive much benefit from a psychological interview because as they relate the problem, they begin to see things of which they had been oblivious. Often, the psychotherapist may help them over their blind spots, and they may then find the solution to their problem. Sometimes the solutions to our problems would be evident if we hadn't "sought many calculations" and complicated them.

ONE PARTICULARLY refreshing observation was made by a gentleman who was sober for more than twenty years. He picked me up at the airport, and as we were en route to the lecture he related the following.

"I'm having a lot of trouble with a newcomer," he said. "He can't seem to put any sober time together. This guy says to me, 'You mean that you haven't had a single drink for over twenty years'?

"'Yep,' I said.

"'What's your trick?' he asked. 'I can't get by without a drink for even a week.'

"I said, 'There's no trick. Every morning, when I wake up, I ask G-d to give me another day of sobriety. At night, before I go to sleep, I thank G-d for having given me another day of sobriety.'

"So this guy says, 'Well, how do you know it was G-d Who gave you a day of sobriety?'

"I looked at him and said, 'You fool. I didn't ask anyone else!'"

What could be simpler?

I'M SURE you've had days when Murphy's Law is in full swing. Anything that can go wrong, does. These are days when we realize we would have been better off pulling the covers over our heads and staying in bed till four in the afternoon.

I had a morning like that in Manhattan. Flat tire, stopped by a police officer for driving ten miles above the limit, not finding an open parking lot, and so on. By noon I was fit to be tied. I felt that the only thing that could get me out of the quicksand was an AA meeting. A call to the local AA office produced no less than four meetings within a six-block radius.

At the meeting I attended, the speaker was a young woman of thirty-five. She had started drinking at twelve and drugging at fifteen. This led to delinquent, decadent behavior. In spite of suffering the consequences of living on the street, she was a slave to her drug addiction.

At twenty-six she found her way to Alcoholics Anonymous and Narcotics Anonymous, and at that time she was nine years clean and sober.

I had heard similar stories countless times, and this one did little for me. But I have never been to a meeting in which I didn't take away something of help. What I took away from this meeting has served me well.

Toward the end of her talk, the woman said, "I must tell you something else before I finish. I am an avid football fan, a Jets fan. I never miss watching a Jets game. One weekend I had to be away, so I asked a friend to record the game on her VCR. When I returned, she handed me the tape and said, 'By the way, the Jets won.'

"I started watching the tape, and it was just horrible. The Jets were being mauled. At halftime they were behind by twenty points. Under other circumstances, I would have been a nervous wreck. I would have been pacing the floor and hitting the refrigerator. But I was perfectly calm, because I knew they were going to win.

"Ever since I turned my life over to G-d, I no longer get uptight when things don't go my way. I may be twenty points behind at halftime, but I know it's going to turn out okay in the end."

This has helped me overcome many difficult times.

IN THE question-and-answer period following a lecture to a group of visiting nurses, one nurse said, "There is one elderly woman I visit regularly. She is a crotchety old woman who is never satisfied with anything I do. 'You made that blood pressure cuff too tight. It's hurting my arm.' When I sponge bathe her, she complains, 'The water is too cold. You're making me shiver.' If I go over the schedule of her medicines, she says, 'You're confusing me. Now I don't know when to take anything.' It's so frustrating. But to top it off, when I leave, she says, 'You're coming back next week, aren't you?' If she doesn't like my service, why does she want me back? She could call the office and request a different nurse."

I was able to solve the problem thanks to something I learned from an octogenarian.

Mrs. Glass had been very active in the ladies auxiliary of my father's congregation. She visited our home frequently, even before I was born. She had watched me grow from my infancy.

When I was an intern, I was called to start an intravenous on Mrs. Glass, who was in her late eighties and was hospitalized because of pneumonia. She had undergone amputation of a leg due to complications of diabetes. She recognized me and we chatted a bit. Then I told her I was going to start her intravenous. "It won't hurt much," I said. "Just a tiny prick of a needle."

Mrs. Glass said, "Foolish child! Let it hurt a lot. Do you think one likes to leave a world that is comfortable?"

It took a bit for Mrs. Glass's words to sink in. What she was saying was that when a person knows his time on earth is running out and he must soon leave it, it is easier if he can see the world as a miserable place. Leaving a pleasant world is much harder.

A perfect vacation is one that has excellent weather for golfing, hiking, swimming, and other outdoor activities, then ends up with the last two days being cold, wet, and dreary. This makes leaving the vacation resort much easier. If the weather is warm and sunny those last few days, it is difficult to leave it to go back to the office.

Mrs. Glass actually wanted to feel that the world was an uncomfortable place. It made the acceptance of the inevitable a bit easier.

The elderly lady who was dissatisfied with everything the nurse did was simply trying to make her departure from the world less painful. She really liked the nurse, as her request "You're coming back, aren't you?" indicated, but in order for her to see the world as a miserable place, she had to complain.

People who care for the elderly are sometimes frustrated by the apparent futility in trying to please them. Mrs. Glass's comment should help them understand that the complaints of these people are not really an expression of dissatisfaction, but a way in which they try to cope with the realization that their time in the world is running out.

LIKE EVERY other person, I do not like to be laden with worries. And like every other person, I usually have enough of them.

When my brother was seriously ill with cancer, I asked a rabbi friend of mine to keep him in his prayers. This white-bearded sage was a kind man who was very wise. I was, therefore, completely taken aback when, on parting, he said to me, "May you be blessed with many worries."

Noting my bewildered expression at this strange blessing, he explained, "It is impossible for a human being to be totally free of worry. Ever since Adam and Eve were expelled from the Garden of Eden, man has been subject to worry.

"Sometimes a person has something so serious on his mind that it obliterates all other concerns. For example, you are so worried about your brother's illness that it occupies your entire mind, and you do not pay attention to the myriad other things in your life.

"When a person has only one worry, that is bad. It means that there is something so terribly distressing bothering him that he doesn't think of anything else. If one has many worries, that means that there is nothing so overwhelmingly bad that it obscures everything else.

"It is not realistic to be without worry. That just does not happen. And it is very bad if a person has only one worry. The best situation, therefore, is for one to have many worries. That means that there is nothing terribly disturbing going on in his life. My blessing to you was that you should have many worries. That means that nothing really bad is on your mind."

Now when I find I am worried about half a dozen things, I am happy.

We all want to have faith. We need to have faith, but sometimes we may find our faith under stress.

After the attack on the World Trade Center, people gathered in churches, synagogues, and mosques to pray. One person interviewed by a television reporter said, "What am I to do? Pray to G-d to care for the souls of those who were killed? If there is a G-d Who is all-powerful, why did He let all those people get killed in the first place?"

This question has been repeatedly asked whenever there is a disaster, whether man-made, like the terrorist attack on the World Trade Center, or from natural causes, such as a tornado, earthquake, or tidal wave that causes loss of life. No one has any logical answer to this question. The faithful can say only that these things are beyond our understanding.

Although I am as incapable of understanding the Divine mysteries as anyone else, I did gain a bit of insight from something I observed in a pediatrician's office.

A mother was sitting with her one-year-old child, who was playing happily with some toys. The doctor, clad in his white coat, entered the waiting room. The baby took one look at the doctor and emitted a shrill scream, clinging to his mother for dear life. The baby remembered only too well what this meant. The man with the white coat is a villain, an evil monster who jabs babies with a sharp needle and makes them hurt and sick for two days.

As the mother carried the baby into the treatment room, the baby cried bitterly and struggled against his mother, biting and kicking her. The mother restrained the baby so that the doctor could administer the immunizing injection. As soon as the doctor withdrew the needle and left, the baby threw its arms around the mother's neck, clutching tightly.

As I observed this, I wondered why the baby was holding

onto its mother for protection. Wasn't she the one who had just collaborated with the villain to let him hurt him? Hadn't she betrayed him? The baby had no way of knowing that the injection would protect him from terrible diseases. The only answer can be that notwithstanding the fact that she was responsible for his getting hurt, the baby knew that she was nevertheless his protector and the one who cared most for him. There was no way he could understand her uncharacteristic behavior, but this did not detract from his trust in her.

The gap between the infant's intellect and his mother's intellect is indeed vast, but the gap between our intellect and the infinite wisdom of G-d is unfathomable. Although like the infant, we cannot understand why He allows us to be hurt, our trust in Him is unshakable.

Whenever I feel like questioning G-d, I am reminded of the scene in the pediatrician's office. Although I cannot understand, it helps me understand why I cannot understand.

ONE DAY at the rehabilitation center, a therapist requested that I see one of his clients. "This fellow has been here for over two weeks," he said, "and he shows no signs of emotion at all. I wonder if he may have a psychiatric problem in addition to his addiction."

The young man was twenty-eight. He was very cooperative in the interview, but in discussing subjects in which some expression of emotion, any emotion, would be normal, there was nothing at all. Among the things he told me was that his father died suddenly when he was ten years old. "I didn't cry. I looked at myself in the mirror and said, 'You're not going to cry.'" In this interview, I did not see signs of any specific psychiatric condition.

The next day, my wife told me that the faucet in the laundry room sink was dripping. I am sufficiently handy to be able to change a washer, but to do so, I needed to turn off the water supply to the faucet. However, the valve was stuck, and I was afraid that if I became more aggressive, I might break a pipe and flood the basement. There was no choice but to call a plumber.

The plumber had no better luck than I did. "This valve is frozen," he said. "It has probably never been turned since the house was built seventy-five years ago. The only thing I can do is shut off the main valve, but that will turn off the water supply to the entire house. It shouldn't be for more than fifteen minutes."

A bit later the plumber came up holding the faucet. "You've got a problem, doc," he said. "It's not the washer. The inside of the faucet is eroded. I'll have to replace the faucet."

"Okay," I said. "There's not much choice."

"I have to go back to the shop to pick up a faucet," he said. "Your water will be off in the whole house for about two hours."

After the new faucet was installed and the main valve turned back on, the plumber opened the faucet, and a gush of rusty water came out with an explosive force and a loud noise. The plumber explained: "When the main valve was turned off, some air got into the pipes. The first time you open any faucet or shower or flush the toilet, you'll get an explosive discharge of water, but after that it'll be okay."

It suddenly became clear to me what had happened with the young man. At age ten, he wanted to protect himself from the painful grief of his father's death. He did not know how to block the isolated emotion of grief, so he did what the plumber did. He shut off the "main valve," turning off *all* emotion. He could feel nothing. After being devoid of feelings for eighteen years, he was afraid to feel anything, even pleasurable emotions. To allow himself now to feel *any* emotion, he would have to turn on the "main valve," but this might result in the emotion coming out with an explosive force that he felt he could not handle. Allowing himself to feel *any* emotion was too threatening, so he kept the "main valve" closed.

Once the problem was identified, we were able to help the young man, offering much reassurance and support to allow him to open his feeling system.

This insight has been very helpful to me. There are many people who seem to be devoid of emotion. This may be because of some occurrence that caused them to turn off their feeling system.

I learned much from this plumber.

You might think that marriage counseling would be a high priority in psychiatric training. After all, so many problems occur in marriage. Just look at the divorce rate in the United States: 40 percent of marriages end in divorce. Someone even quipped, "The leading cause of divorce is marriage." Strange, I received no instruction at all about marriage or spouse abuse.

I was left on my own to figure out how to handle marital strife. I read some books on the subject. But one of the best insights came from a patient who told me that at one point, his marriage was in deep trouble.

"My wife and I had frequent spats," he said. "I never wanted to yield. It was a matter of pride. I was right even if I was wrong.

"Then one day it occurred to me that if I win an argument, that means that my wife lost it. But I didn't want to be married to a loser, so we stopped fighting."

Perhaps it was still a matter of pride that he did not want to be married to a loser, but it is certainly a much healthier result of pride than on insisting on being a winner.

Here's something I learned that was very important in my psychiatric practice. I learned it from a patient, and that patient was *me*.

I received my psychiatric training in 1960, before much was known about the chemistry of emotions. The institute where I trained was wedded to Freudian psychology. We were taught that all depressions were due to a loss of some sort. The reasoning went like this: A loss results in being depressed. Therefore, every depression is due to a loss. But what if the depressed person had not sustained a loss? Never mind. He did suffer a loss, but was unaware of it. His *subconscious* was aware of the loss.

We were taught that the depression that not infrequently follows childbirth is because the woman has *lost* the pregnancy. But this is no loss. She very much wanted the child, and was so happy with it. Well, the reasoning went, her *conscious* mind was happy with the baby, but to her *subconscious,* delivering the baby was like losing a part of her body. I hate to admit that I bought into this theory.

In my second year of training, I became depressed. I couldn't think of what I might have lost. As the depression grew worse, I consulted one of my instructors. After listening to me, he said, "Abe, are you taking any medications?"

"Just something for hay fever, a decongestant," I said.

"Why don't you just stop the medication and let's see what happens." I stopped the medication, and within two weeks my depression disappeared. I later noted that one of the side effects of this medication could be depression.

I returned to my instructor. "What about the theory that depression is always due to a loss, either a conscious or subconscious one?"

My instructor smiled. "There is no greater tragedy than a good theory being disproved by a fact."

Ever since then psychiatry has advanced. It is now common knowledge that many depressions are the result of an imbalance in the body's chemistry. I found this out the hard way.

50

THE RABBINIC INFLUENCE

People often pose two questions to me: "Were patients ever turned off by your appearance as a rabbi?" and "Did being a rabbi influence the way you practiced psychiatry?"

As far as my appearance is concerned, I never considered it a problem, and perhaps that is why patients did not consider it a problem.

One time my appearance was a factor. I attended a meeting of Alcoholics Anonymous, and the speaker was a young woman. Among the things she said was, "When I was admitted to St. Francis Hospital, I was told that a psychiatrist would come to talk to me. I said, 'He can talk all he wants to. I'm not talking to any shrink.'

"I was sitting on the floor in my room when this guy with a long beard walks in, wearing a white coat and a beanie on his head, and sits down on the floor opposite me. I thought he was one of the patients. We struck up a conversation for an hour, and I told him things that I would never tell a psychiatrist."

So much for the effect of my appearance.

I believe that my training as a rabbi and my study of Torah did have an effect on my relationship with people. I came to believe that there is good in every person, but often it is concealed, so much so that the person is unaware of the good within him.

A number of years ago, I began a small rehabilitation program in Israel for ex-convicts who had been imprisoned for drug-related crimes. In a session with the first group of clients, I pointed out that there is a natural resistance to avoid damaging an object of beauty. Inasmuch as everyone knows that drugs are damaging, there should have been greater resistance to their taking drugs. The reason they did not have this resistance was because they had never considered themselves to be worthy and beautiful. I said that long-term recovery depends on developing self-esteem, so that one would not want to damage himself.

One of the ex-convicts said, "How can you expect me to have self-esteem. I'm thirty-four years old, and sixteen of those thirty-four years have been spent in prison. When I get out of prison, no one will give me a job. When the social worker tells my family that I will be released in ninety days, they are very unhappy. I am a burden and an embarrassment to them. They wish I would stay in jail forever or even die. How am I supposed to have self-esteem?"

"Avi," I said to him, "have you ever seen a display of diamonds in a jewelry store window? Those diamonds are scintillatingly beautiful and worth hundreds of thousands of dollars. Do you know what they looked like when they were brought out of the diamond mine? They looked like ugly, dirty pieces of glass, which anyone would think worthless.

"At the diamond mine, there is a *meivin* (expert) who scrutinizes the ore. He may pick up a "dirty piece of glass" and marvel at the precious gem that lies within. He sends it to the processing plant, and it emerges as a magnificently beautiful, shining diamond.

"No one can put any beauty into a dirty piece of glass. The

beauty of the diamond was always there, but it was concealed by layers of material that covered it. The processing plant removed these layers to reveal the beauty of the diamond. They did not create the beauty; they just exposed it.

"I may not be a *meivin* on diamonds, Avi," I said, "but I am a *meivin* on people. You have a beautiful soul within you, but it has been covered with layers of ugly behavior. We will help you get rid of those layers and reveal the beauty of your soul."

Avi stayed in the program for several months, then was in a transitional facility for eight months. After leaving, he found a job and remained free of drugs.

One day, Annette, the administrator of the transitional program, received a call from a family whose elderly mother had died, leaving an apartment full of furniture for which they had no use. They offered to donate the furniture to the rehabilitation program. Annette called Avi. "I have no way of getting that furniture here," she told him. "Could you help us?" Avi assured her that he would get a truck and bring the furniture.

Two days later, Avi called Annette. "I am at the apartment," he said, "but there is no point in bringing the furniture. It is old and worn out."

"I don't want to disappoint the family, Avi," Annette said. "Bring it here. Perhaps we can salvage some of it."

Avi loaded the truck and brought the furniture to the facility, which was on the second floor of a building. As he dragged an old sofa up the stairs, an envelope fell from the cushions. It contained five thousand shekels (approximately fourteen hundred dollars). This was money of whose existence no one knew, and the rule of "finders keepers" could easily have been applied, especially by someone who used to break into a house for ten shekels.

Avi called Annette and told her about the money. "That's the family's money," she said. "Call them and tell them." The family graciously donated the money to the rehabilitation program.

On a subsequent visit to Israel, I met Avi at a function of the rehabilitation program, and that is when Annette told me the story about the five thousand shekels. I said to Avi, "Do you remember our first meeting when you did not know how you could ever have self-esteem? I told you that there was a soul, a beautiful diamond within you. Many people who never stole a penny would have simply pocketed the money. What you did was truly exceptional, and shows the beauty of the 'diamond' within you."

Several months later, Avi affixed a bronze plaque on the door of the rehabilitation center. It read Diamond Processing Center.

That is what I mean by "there is good in everyone." It just needs to be revealed.

ABOUT THE AUTHOR

Abraham J. Twerski, M.D.
Founder and Medical Director Emeritus
Gateway Rehabilitation Center

Dr. Twerski, an ordained rabbi, held a pulpit until 1959 when he graduated from Marquette University Medical School and went on to complete his psychiatric residency at the University of Pittsburgh Western Psychiatric Institute. For twenty years, he served as clinical director of the department of psychiatry at St. Francis Hospital, Pittsburgh, and was an associate professor of psychiatry at the University of Pittsburgh's School of Medicine. He has been awarded honorary degrees from St. Vincent's College, Duquesne University, and Indiana University of Pennsylvania based on his scientific contributions and community efforts.

Dr. Twerski stems from a long line of Chassidic rabbis, of the Chernobyl and Sanz dynasties, and traces his ancestry to the Baal Shem Tov, founder of the Chassidic movement.

The author of more than sixty books, Dr. Twerski has been featured in hundreds of magazines, newspapers, and other publications. Among his many books are *Living Each Day*, a book containing daily inspirational messages; *Twerski on Prayer*; *Lights Along the Way*, a commentary on *Mesillas Yesharim* (*Path of the Just*); *Angels Don't Leave Footprints*; *Life's Too Short*; *Ten Steps to Being Your Best* on issues of self-esteem; and *Getting Up When You're Down* on depression and related conditions.

Two of Dr. Twerski's books, *When Do the Good Things Start?* and *Waking Up Just in Time*, which have been translated into several languages, were written in collaboration with the late Charles Schulz, creator of the *Peanuts* comic strip, and the *Peanuts* characters appear on their pages. His mastery in storytelling can be seen in *Not Just Stories*, a collection of inspiring Chassidic tales. *Happiness and the Human Spirit* is Dr. Twerski's take on spirituality. Also authored by Dr. Twerski is *A Formula for Proper Living*, a guide to psychologically sound living based on Torah sources.

His popular weekly "Seeking Solutions" column in the *Hamodia* newspaper has resulted in two volumes of *Dear Rabbi, Dear Doctor,* providing guidance on a wide spectrum of problems. His book *Addictive Thinking* is a primer in the field of addiction. Dr. Twerski courageously pioneered awareness of spouse abuse among Jews in *The Shame Borne in Silence,* and addictive gambling in *Compulsive Gambling: More than Dreidel.*

Without a Job, Who Am I? offers a system of support designed to help individuals develop and sustain a true sense of self-worth and identity after being shaken by professional or economic upheaval.

Dr. Twerski has lectured extensively on chemical dependency and other topics such as stress, self-esteem, and spirituality.

In addition, he has traveled the world as a spokesperson for recovery on behalf of the millions who have achieved it and with goals that inspire, encourage, and challenge those still finding their way.

Dr. Twerski first opened Gateway Rehabilitation Center in 1972 as a twenty-eight-day alcohol and drug-dependence treatment center. A 2008 James W. West, M.D., Quality Improvement Award winner, Gateway Rehab also has been named one of the nation's "top twelve rehabilitation programs" in a survey conducted by *Forbes* magazine and called one of the "best treatment centers" in both *Rehab* magazine and the *100 Best Treatment Centers Guide to Addiction Care*. Gateway has since expanded to a network of facilities in Pennsylvania and Ohio, and its staff provides services to more than fifteen hundred clients daily. An expanded Youth and Family Center became operative in August 2012.

The following is a list of Dr. Twerski's remarkable achievements.

- Received **50 Years of Service Award** from the Allegheny County Medical Society, 2008
- Featured in the book *Pittsburgh Born, Pittsburgh Bred* as one of **"500 of the most memorable Pittsburghers** who have shaped the region and the world in the past 250 years," 2008
- Received the **Michael Q. Ford Journalism Award** from the National Association of Addiction Treatment Providers (NAATP), 2006
- Received Gateway Rehabilitation Center's inaugural Hope Award, now known as the **Twerski Hope Award,** 2005
- Received the **Nelson J. Bradley Lifetime Achievement Award**, given annually by the NAATP to an individual

whose lifetime has been committed to furthering the cause of addiction treatment, 2002

- Received **Health Care Hero Lifetime Achievement Award,** presented by the *Pittsburgh Business Times*, Allegheny County Medical Society, and the Western Pennsylvania Hospital Council, 2001
- Received the Catholic Charities of Pittsburgh's **Caritas Award for Service,** 1998
- Received the American Psychiatric Association's **Oskar Pfister Award,** 1998
- Received the Pennsylvania Medical Society's **Distinguished Service Award**, the society's greatest honor given to an individual for his or her dedication to work in the chemical dependency field, 1997
- Named a **"Real Pittsburgher"** by *Pittsburgh Magazine*, 1991
- Earned citation for **Contribution to the Integration of Religion and the Behavioral Sciences,** 1980
- Received the **Martin Luther King Citizen's Award,** 1975